EDITED BY EVELYN McDONNELL

Rock She Wrote: Women Write About Rock, Pop, and Rap
(coedited with Ann Powers)

Stars Don't Stand Still in the Sky: Music and Myth
(coedited with Karen Kelly)

Army of She

EVELYN McDONNELL

ARMY OF SHE

Icelandic, Iconoclastic, Irrepressible Björk

ATRANDOM.COM

NEW YORK

Grateful acknowledgment is made to Quest Management for permission to include lyrics from "Hunter," "5 Years," "Birthday" and "Immature." Reprinted by permission of Quest Management

ISBN: 0-8129-9150-8

24689753

First Edition

TO

MUSIC

LOVERS

Contents

PREFATORY EPISODE:

In which the narrator explains

the whole "e-Björk" concept, and

falls in love with a sound

Björk Gudmundsdóttir was about twenty years into her career before I liked her. This places me somewhere in between the two groups of people most likely to be reading these words: those of you who heard about the numerous awards and award nominations for her role in the film *Dancer in the Dark,* promptly said to yourselves, "What is this thing called Björk? And why is she wearing a swan?", and conducted the appropriate web searches; and those of you who are Björkophiles, collectors of her every white-label remix and guest vocal appearance, connoisseurs of all things Björk—even e-books by comparative greenhorns.

This is not a biography. No interviews were conducted especially for it, no new information worth bragging about is revealed, long blocks of time and pieces of work (those excruciatingly jaunty Sugarcubes tracks) are completely skipped over. An excellent, detailed, thoughtful overview of the artist's life up until 1996 has already been presented by English journalist Martin Aston in the book *Björkgraphy.* Although it is somewhat out of date and sadly out of print, if that's the kind of thing you're looking for, then this is another perfect illustration of why AmazonNoble.com will never replace the beautifully musty haven of used bookstores. Turn off the computer and dust off those dustjackets!

This is something else: yes, a new hyped new media new technology with a cute marketing name that makes e-fficient, e-conomic use of that ubiquitous electronic-age, neologism-friendly, monosyllabic prefix—ladies and gentlemen, an e-book. I think of it as an endeavor as retro as techno (a very Björkian balance, by the way: see E-pisode 3), the resuscitation and revitalization of a genre that had become ghettoized as the sole province of (gasp) scholarly types, the return of the thumbsucker special: an e-ssay. My say, on why a woman-child from the island nation of Iceland is the most interesting, the most important, the most innovative, and the most engaging musical star of our precipitous, capricious times.

If you don't know a thing about Björk except her gutbucket performance in *Dancer in the Dark,* then hopefully this piece of writing will show you the wild landscape of her pop, fashion, and moving-image forest without knocking you out on the pesky trees of detail. If you know everything about Björk, then maybe this will change your mind: put her into perspectives you hadn't thought of, make you reevaluate aspects of her life you had taken for granted, give you some arguments with which to justify your obsession to concerned parents—make you more crazy about her than ever.

It may have taken me twenty years, but I'm a fan—a skeptical critic converted by music so spectacularly intimate, it feels like breath. I think of "Bachelorette," a love song from the 1997 album *Homogenic* that has a tango bassline and Puccini-worthy lyrics of passion (by Icelandic poet Sjón), and it instantly lodges in my throat, residing midway between pulmonary central and nerve headquarters, until I want to exhale it out or suck its oxygen in from scalp to toe. A song can inhabit you, until you expel it in voice or let it send you spinning—sing or dance along.

In August 1997 I interviewed Björk for a cover story for the music magazine *Request,* published when *Homogenic* was "released," as the saying goes (as if it had been held captive). I was at that point at least curious and respectful of her work, having gotten over my early annoyance at the bewitchingly pedophilic appeal of her childlike manner. And I was growing more in love with *Homogenic* with each headphones listen as my plane flew into Iceland. My advance copy of the album (ultimate rock-crit perk) had arrived the same day I took off from Minneapolis, and so I spent the flight cramming to understand her.

Music can mark time, and vice versa. The process can be as simple as *Big Chill* nostalgia: We like a song because we heard it when we were falling in love, or having a good time at a party, or lost in delirium on the dance floor. When we hear the song later, even years later, it takes us back to those memories: It's a trigger, a madeleine, a remembrance of flings past. Or the connection can be more serpentine. Events and melodies can influence each other, the tone of a song becomes the color of our experience, we adjust the pace of our bodies to the rhythm that repeats itself in our head, then suddenly we're soaring up the road in a burst of strings or crashing like cymbals into bed.

What do I mean by "we," *kemosabe?* I certainly don't intend it as the royal we. I suppose I'm hoping it's a communal "we," that I'm describing a basic human experience, that music really is the universal language. Or maybe I'm just speaking for my tribe—the "certain brand of people," including herself, that Björk told *Flaunt* magazine she was defending with her portrayal of Selma in *Dancer in the Dark:* one of those "people who hears music all the time in their head, from like, one year old—they may be with ten other people but all they're hearing is this kind of soundtrack."

Homogenic quickly became part of my soundtrack, beginning on the plane as it wheeled over the Arctic and I stared out the window at Greenland's white, white glaciers reflected in blue, blue waters, a vision from a million TV screens that was even more impressively Technicolor in real life, a moving landscape being scored for me by Björk's equally vivid and dramatic soundscapes. This was a repeat of a primal experience for me: Ever since I was a kid riding in a car on cross-country summer vacations, I've sat looking out of windows with songs in my head, musical daydreaming between destinations. I've loved music ever since I can remember; say three sentences to me and I'll find a song lyric in them, I'm that "certain brand of people."

In 1997, musical daydreaming was something I repeated over and over, traveling out of my Manhattan home a dozen times in as many months. The year had started with an uprooting: I had moved to Florence to be with my husband, only to have him kick me out two weeks later. Temporarily homeless, I traipsed from Belize to Michigan to L.A. to Reykjavík, learning to reanchor myself to the music in my head wherever my hat found itself.

So the opening lines of *Homogenic* struck a nerve: "If travel is searching / and home has been found / I'm not stopping," Björk sings in a tremulous whisper over a rippling electronic drum and warbling, synthesized strings. "Hunter" blends the aching live sound of the Icelandic String Octet (orchestrated by Eumir Deodato, the Brazilian Quincy Jones, best known for the early-seventies hit "2001: A Space Odyssey"), Yasuhiro "Coba" Kobayashi's mournful accordion, and stuttering computer beats and beeps programmed by Brit brainiac Mark Bell. Tying the whole shebang together is Björk's vocal: full of reverberating menace and trepidation on the verses, then bursting into full-throated confession, layers of her voice pitching next to each other then cascading together. The music swells like stormy waves, then eases back, but each crash is a little more threatening, each ebb more fragile, until the song fades out uncertainly, a threat not delivered but not rescinded either, not stopping. The lyrics hint at a failed relationship; it's not clear if the singer is hunting for someone new, or someone old. The rest of the album, you're not sure if you're in her sights.

I'd never heard anything like it, really. The production showed Björk's steeping in the cutting edge of electronic dance-music culture, her embrace of techno futurism, her time spent pulling all-nighters in London clubs. But the emotion was ancient, deeply human—the voice of what hippie types like to call "an old soul." It was a song I instantly wanted to share with my most avant-garde friends and my showtune-loving mother. Like its multinational, multigenerational players, it was music that seemed impossible to tribalize, to fit into a tidy section at the record store—or, lord help us, an American radio format. "I think my music is world music," Björk told me later that day in a café in Reykjavík. "But I'd be lying if I wouldn't say I'm being ironic about it," she added, smiling her "I'm light-years ahead of you" imp smile.

Music critics, like myself, are infamous for our penchant for categories. We tend to confuse our job with zoologists', to want to make sense of the world by organizing taxonomies, then slotting everything into its accorded genus and species. We think this will help people understand the mysterious appeal of music. We're often right. But sometimes we forget that people want to appreciate, not destroy, the mystery. Sometimes we replace description with conscription, variations with labels, people with stereotypes.

Up until *Homogenic,* I myself had used the prevalent critical category for Björk's uncategorizable amalgam of styles: "quirky."

There was nothing quirky about "Hunter."

EPISODE 2

In which the narrator and our heroine play queen of the mountain

Not surprisingly for an artist who hails from a volcanic island nation, two of Björk's best songs are about making pilgrimages up mountaintops. In the first, a fantasy of renunciation called "Hyper-ballad," from her 1995 album, *Post,* she's Moses: Every day, she goes to the cliff and hurls objects over the edge—car parts, bottles, cutlery. On occasion, she envisions throwing herself off: "Imagine what my body would sound like / slamming against those rocks." Having thus unburdened herself, she can go about the business of having a relationship.

In "Alarm Call," a song on *Homogenic,* she goes to the mountaintop not to denounce human foibles, but to place a boom box. From that stereo, Björk promises to broadcast music that will "free the human race from suffering." A tall order, but as the song unfolds—a bubbling mix of synthesizer exclamations and belted aphorisms—I realize, if anyone can do it, Björk can.

This may come as a surprise to musicians who have suffered

the slings and arrows of a bad review, but the calling of a critic is not necessarily different from that of an artist. Some pundits may see themselves up there decreeing commandments, but I prefer Björk's later mission: to spread the good word of good music. This is the calling that keeps the music critic (arguably, a contradiction in terms) from feeling like a killjoy—that makes her feel the opposite, a breedjoy. Music is a gift, an offering to the world, and I want to offer you Björk, to take her up on the mountaintop, turn the volume to 11, let that mix of strings, beats, and volcanic voice disseminate over the valley, let you hear her without the everyday baggage of car parts and cutlery.

But having yet to find a mountaintop with the proper acoustics, I'm plugging into the Internet.

EPISODE 3

In which our heroine discusses

"outrageous change"

In lieu of reciting her whole life story, here are some telling facts and anecdotes, signposts for discovery of this thing called Björk:

• She had her first hit single in Iceland at age eleven, when—as a child prodigy encouraged by her mother—she recorded a self-titled debut album of pop covers, traditional Icelandic songs, and one instrumental composition of her own.

• When she was thirteen, she shaved off her eyebrows and played drums in an all-girl punk band named Spit & Snot. (Try that, Britney.) "We believed boys are crap, they're only good for shagging," she told me.

• When her band Kukl [www.southern.com/southern/band/ KUKLL] played on Icelandic TV, Björk appeared with eyebrows shaved and pregnant stomach bared. At least one viewer suffered a heart attack.

• She gave birth to her son, Sindri, when she was nineteen. "Because I was brought up around loads of kids with a massive family—where the attitude was you get pregnant, you put it under your arm, and you keep on doing what you're doing— I never thought having a kid was a big deal."

• She got a black tattoo on her arm in 1981; it's an Icelandic compass, taken from Viking mythology. A close friend has the same tattoo. "We didn't have to talk, we were so in tune."

• The Sugarcubes, her first international hit band, evolved out of a cooperative of Dada-inspired poets and artists named Medusa.

• In Britain, she remains signed to the same independent label, One Little Indian, that the Sugarcubes first signed with in 1987.

• She is Europe's most renowned female pop star of the past decade—arguably, its brightest star of any gender.

• The British tabloids have long tracked her every liaison with other artists (Tricky, Goldie, Howie B, Stéphane Sednaoui, and so on).

• She's a futuristic pop artist who has toured with such old-fashioned instruments as harpsichord and accordion.

• She made global headlines in 1996, when she physically attacked a TV reporter in Bangkok's airport—while the cameras were rolling.

• After being awarded Best Actress at the Cannes Film Festival for her performance in *Dancer in the Dark,* she announced she was giving up acting.

• She is not nearly as winningly daft as she often seems (or is portrayed).

Björk is an actress. At a press conference for *Dancer in the Dark* at the New York Film Festival on September 20, 2000, a male audience member launched into a long congratulatory speech in which, among other accolades, he likened Björk's presence there to the appearance a year earlier of Hillary Swank (who went on to win an Oscar for her role in *Boys Don't Cry*). Björk quickly hunkered up to the mike, a strange smile on her face. "Who's Hillary Swank?" she asked, her thick eyebrows an arrow, a picture of naïveté.

Björk is, in fact, smart and mischievous. "She claims she's not an actress, but she certainly knows how to create a persona," observes New York City–based avant-garde harpist Zeena Parkins, with whom Björk collaborated on her 2001 release *Vespertine.* "This is a woman who knows how to use a camera." Björk's naïve act is classic feminine guile: She knows the power of seeming accommodating to win her way, is happy to be a tabula rasa for sycophants rather than an uppity bitch—but, as *Dancer* director Lars von Trier learned all too well when she walked off the film set one weekend, she is in the end always willing to assert herself. Her greatest gift may be trust; woe to he who doesn't return the offer.

Her meekness and awkwardness—she's the ultimate glamorous geek—hide the fact she is actually sussing strangers out. She obviously knows how to play men. Women, I suspect, are more of a challenge for her, and less frequent collaborators. When she and I meet, I feel like she doesn't know what to make of me for most of the time we're together. Björk and I spend a couple hours together, both friendly and polite. She seems very guarded about anything personal, and eventually admits, "Since I've been doing this since I was so young, I think subconsciously I quickly learned to draw a line between private and public. That doesn't mean when I do an interview I'm lying. To me [the public and private are] two separate things. It would be a lie if I were to start talking about things to you that I talk about only to my closest friends." (This is far nicer than the answer she gave *Paper* magazine around the same time, when it got nosy: "I'd be ashamed to do this interview in Icelandic. But I can do it in English because it's the language of cheap things: Small talk, clichés, fashion.")

So I scrupulously avoid pushing any privacy-issue buttons, and Björk feeds me wonderfully original, intellectual quotes; she's an interviewer's dream, a virtuoso of colorful anecdotes and metaphors. Still, I don't feel like we break through to any real connection until exhaustion and endurance (the interview takes place in and around the photo shoot, a trying setup for everyone involved) breed a touch of trust, a bond of patience.

We all climb into a minivan for the half-hour trek to the Blue Lagoon, a spa created by the runoff from a geothermal power plant; steamy azure waters amid dark lava rocks make for a splendid photo op. On the outskirts of Reykjavík, Björk softly points out a modest home with a red roof and two windows around the door, like eyes on a face. It looks like a one-room schoolhouse, alone on a plain. She murmurs so quietly in her Icelandic accent I don't understand what she's telling me at first: that it's the house she lived in from age six to ten. "The roof leaked, so when it rained we had to have a bucket," she says, then adds wryly, like she's talking about a recording session: "Low budget." I look again and picture the house's interior painted purple and crowded with people, the friends and followers of her mother's communal lifestyle. I imagine growing up there, surrounded and alone, a little girl next to her little house, twirling around in the big outdoors. I'm surprised that the careful recluse has shown me something so intimate, and grateful.

Much has been made, by Björk among others, of her unconventional upbringing. Her parents divorced before she was three, and she was raised primarily by her artist mother, Hildur Hauksdóttir, as well as by her father, Gudmundur Gunnarsson, grandparents, and various stepparents and friends. She's said that since she was five, it was she who helped her absentminded mother cross streets, not vice versa—seems the child and adult have long coexisted in Björk. "I was allowed to do whatever I wanted," she told me as we rode past her old stomping grounds. "There were no restrictions. Once, I wore my duvet cover to school. Then again, there was no discipline, so I had to bring myself up. Living in a small village, okay, your mother may be trippy—I don't mean in a drug way, I mean she may be painting clouds on the ceiling, or running around naked when you're supposed to be having dinner. But I had a hundred people who were like family in the town, so I could just go to Gran's for a solid meal, or if I wanted discipline."

At times Björk has described this unconventional rearing as if it were a burden she has had to overcome. At age eighteen she became "a rebel anti-hippie," she told Jon Savage in *Interview;* some of her most brilliantly derisive diatribes have been aimed at people stuck in the sixties. Ultimately, however, she's grateful for the way she was allowed to grow up—or not grow up, as the case may be. "I had a really wild upbringing, which I think is the best upbringing anyone could have," she also told Savage. "She would have out-of-body experiences on top of the traffic lights," Björk said to me of her mother. "She's brilliant, she's really proud." Bohemian households such as Hildur's are often breeding grounds for extraordinary talents. Björk is the most successful of a whole generation of little girls who were thankfully never told that they should be seen and not heard, such as original art punk Ari Up of London's Slits, stepsisters Kristin Hersh and Tanya Donelly of Rhode Island's Throwing Muses, and San Francisco's Barbara Manning.

Björk was encouraged artistically from an early age. Her mother and grandmother are painters. Her stepfather, Saevar Arnason, is a rock guitarist known, painfully enough, as "Iceland's Eric Clapton." "I've always sung, since I was a kid," she said in a profile of her filmed by Bravo TV in 1997. "It's always been my natural reaction to things." Björk began attending Baramusik-skola Reykjavíkur music school at five, studying flute and piano: Few pop stars have such a solid rooting in classical music and music theory. Not that Björk enjoyed it. "I couldn't handle the obsession with the past, the whole dead-person cliché," she told me. "I had these fierce arguments with the headmaster; we'd have these screaming one-on-ones. At the same time I fought against it, I was the one who stayed longest at the school. It was sort of a love-hate relationship. I felt fiercely about making music today, making new songs—stop being so tied to the past and trying to imitate something that's gone. I liked the sessions where the kids would sit in a room, and one person would have a flute, and one would have instruments they didn't even know, and you could do whatever you wanted. But then again I was brought up with hip-pies, so I couldn't stand going nowhere fast. I'm really fierce against that. I like this century, I can relate to it more easily."

I suspect Björk was also not interested in becoming sucked into a world that could be upper-class, elitist, pretentious, high-falutin. "I make music for everyone, not for VIP or educated peo-ple," she told Bravo. The singer is adamantly, even sentimentally, more connected to her proletarian heritage than to a bohemian one. Before she became a rock star, she worked at a fish factory, an antique shop, and a Coca-Cola bottling plant. Her father (whom she took to the 2000 Golden Globe Awards) is an electri-cian, and she frequently compares her job to his: She probably prefers the term *artisan* to *artist*. This down-to-earthness comes from growing up in a small country, where you can't much get away with putting on airs. "It's like a gang," she said. "There's only 280,000 of us. They're in my team." She has been described ad nauseam as an odd character: "elfin," "spritelike," "quirky," etc. But Björk's highly developed imagination is balanced by a strong pragmatism; she's a bit of a frontier gal. "There's a stubborn kind of self-sufficiency in Iceland. You've got be self-made. If your car breaks down, you fix it yourself. My family still hunts for meat, for bird and fish. We're so close to nature."

Iceland is at once an isolated, desolate island and a country of unmatched natural beauty and warm humanity. Top among its remarkable characteristics is the fact that due to its high northern latitude (65 degrees), half the year the sun barely sets, the other half it barely rises. "There's not much difference in temperature, but the difference in light is enormous," Björk told me. "In summer you're very social, and in winter you're quite introverted. You do a lot of work inside your house. I like that, it suits my character." Geologically, it is also a land of extremes, of fire (hot lava, geysers, and other geothermal wonders) and ice (glaciers, icecaps, and lots of snow). "Icelandic people tend to be quite passionate about things," said Björk. "It's all or nothing. There's no understatements or maybes. People that are leveled and balanced, I get humble when I'm next to them. I can't believe it's possible."

Most of the country is uninhabited; it has the largest wilderness areas in Europe. The only highway skirts the coast, missing the interior completely. The geologically infant land is still being formed by the movements of the earth's crust. Waterfalls, volcanoes, earthquakes—it's a continually unfolding drama. In 1963, a whole island, Surtsey, was born from one eruption. A decade later, a volcano buried one third of the town of Heimaey. "I think what's most Icelandic about this album is energy-wise, it's kind of raw," Björk said to me, discussing *Homogenic*. "I was in a helicopter yesterday going in the glacier, through the canyons, real fast. It was like the last scene in *Star Wars* One, going whooosh. I was crying my eyes out, because this is me."

The Irish monks who first inhabited Iceland weren't exactly destined to populate it; that was up to the Vikings from Norway who arrived a short time later, in the ninth century. These infamous warriors were quickly tamed by Iceland's severity and became fabled yarn spinners instead. (What else do you do when the lights are out for months on end, and then, later, your Danish occupiers outlaw song and dance?) Much of our modern knowledge of ancient Europe is derived from the Icelandic sagas. These were passed on by Icelandic-style griots whose deliveries are echoed in Björk's unique way of singing, relying on rhythm and volume for emphasis and expression as much as European melody and harmony for order.

"This is a nation of storytelling," Björk told me. "The Germans, Scandinavians, and Irish come here to ask us what happened, because we wrote everything down. We don't really have painting, we don't really have music. It all goes to storytelling and information. And of course this is the age of information, so we have some of the best Internet companies in the world." More books are read per capita by Icelanders than by any other nationality in the world. All this literacy has made Icelanders a particularly erudite, forward-thinking lot. Then again, in an embarrassing prohibition-era leftover, beer was not legalized until 1989.

Icelanders may have been enjoying a life of the mind, but their physical existence has been much harsher. For most of the last millennium, their economy subsisted on farming and fish, they were repeatedly rocked by natural disasters, and they were under the rule of Denmark. World War II changed all that, and Iceland has quickly made up for lost time, rushing to embrace new technology. "My grandfather was brought up in a mud house: no electricity, no nothing," Björk said. "It's been a very dramatic change in one century." As political scientist Björk astutely pointed out, this future-shock vertigo gives Iceland more in common with the second and third worlds than with Europe and the United States:

"Those countries, they all had three or four hundred years to adapt to Western civilization, they had industrialization and all that shit. But all the other countries, like in South America and Asia, they became Western civilized in fifty years. They took an aggressive shortcut. Iceland was a colony until 1944. We've been independent for fifty years. Before that, we were living in the Middle Ages. A lot of literature from South America, or a lot of films from Asia, they talk about having one foot in nature, in the mud, in mythology, and the other foot in mobile phones. I used to think that sort of thing was special for Iceland. But I realized I was being smitten by this whole [idea] of London or New York being the center of the world, this white-male, Western civilization, blah blah blah [idea] saying this is normal and the rest is weird. I realized that the USA and them are the minority, and the rest of the world has gone through the same in the last hundred years: an outrageous change. In my music, talking about mountains but talking about ghetto blasters, and talking about the wind in my hair but being in a club disco dancing, it seems like I'm the odd one out, but actually . . ."

In other words, a song such as "The Modern Things" has more in common with the postcolonialist magic realism of Latin American writers Gabriel García Márquez and Carlos Fuentes than with rock 'n' roll. In this fanciful track from her 1995 album *Post,* Björk imagines that "cars and such have always existed / they've just been waiting in a mountain" to come out and make themselves useful. "Sometimes I think nature and techno is the same word, it just depends on if it's [said in the] past or future," she told me. "One thousand years ago you'd look at a log cabin in the forest, and that would be techno. And now it's nature. There's the security of the past, and nostalgia, and Granny, and having hot cocoa. And then there's the other, which is learning new technology, not knowing what's going to happen in a week: Will I be happy, will I keep my job, will I be in love forever? It's a balance between those two."

During my stay, I didn't get to see a lot of Iceland. Elektra, Björk's American record company, had arranged the flight for a mere twenty-four-hour visit; it was intimated to me that people didn't want me snooping around Björk's backyard too long. In fact, I could have changed the ticket but ultimately decided that a day trip to Iceland was very jet-setty glamorous. Besides, in the summer, a day in Iceland counts as two days elsewhere.

With the exceptions of the bus ride to and from the airport and the excursion to the Blue Lagoon, I spent the time in Reykjavík; I didn't experience the wild terrain that's the heart of the Icelandic experience. But the city, while sparklingly clean and full of small, cozy, walkable European streets and expensive stores and restaurants, has its share of native wildness. For one, the hot water that came out of the hotel's showers was pumped straight from a natural pool just beneath the earth's crust; all homes there get their heat and hot water from this geothermal resource. My favorite thing about Iceland is the public pools, filled with mineral-rich water and also featuring multitemperatured hot tubs; you can swim in them outdoors year-round, even in the long, cold, dark winter.

Icelanders are party animals. All that extreme weather, the extended light and dark—wouldn't you be? If you're partying until the break of dawn, and it takes months for dawn to finally break . . . you get the picture. We—the photographer, her brother, and I—went out our one night with some locals. They were intense talkers and intense drinkers. I've hung with a lot of rock bands and know some pretty raucous poets in New York, but these guys had taken the bohemian ideal of living life fully as a do-or-die mission. I'd never seen anyone loosen up so seriously. They scared me a little. "People who go there think the Icelanders are really stressed out," Björk told *Interview* magazine in 1995. "They're not, but their energy is on ten."

Björk is, as she would say, "fiercely proud" of being from Iceland. For all the reasons stated above—its wild climate and ecology, its intellectualism, its headlong rush into the future—her home has undoubtedly made her who she is. But it's no utopia. The nation remains overwhelmingly Scandinavian, and Icelanders routinely trace their lineage back several centuries, if not all the way to the Vikings; *Homogenic* indeed. That's what Björk means when she says she has "genes that go twelve hundred years back being what I am, with my nose, my eyes, whatever."

But Björk does not look like a typical Icelander; she does not have the requisite blond hair and blue eyes. According to Martin Aston, she has an occasionally recurring Inuit gene to thank for her dark, Asiatic looks; it seems the Vikings had the odd encounter with Greenland neighbors. When I asked people in Reykjavík to explain Björk's un-Scandinavian appearance, they confirmed this theory—although some whispered this hint of miscegenation to me, as if it were a dark secret. When Björk was growing up, kids called her China Girl.

Icelanders profess to being staunchly unracist. And increasingly, Björk's not the only "China girl" there: many Icelanders adopted Vietnamese orphans, and lately there has been an influx of Thai immigrants. Björk ascribes her own national pride to the experience brought about by gathering, not segregating, tribes. "For a lot of people nationalism is a bad thing, because it's about the past. What's beautiful about modern days is that all over the world, more and more people are having similar lifestyles. And because of that, our identity becomes even stronger, because the opposites meet in an even more fierce way. I go to London, and I've never been so Icelandic. When I lived here, I didn't even think about it."

And yet, Björk clearly had a reason for titling the album that marked her return to home after a word for sameness, for purity. And it was precisely a less homogenic world Björk sought, and sucked up, when she left Iceland. "I think what attracts me and turns me on is extremes," Björk told me. "And that's probably the best thing about me and the worst thing about me. I like very pure things, like harps. And I like Iceland's being as Iceland as possible. But then I like being on Times Square and being surrounded with at least fifty nationalities. I believe in both."

After the debut album Björk recorded at eleven went gold, she could have made another one. But being a child-star prodigy was not for her; she was no Debbie Gibson, or Christina Aguilera. Instead, she cut her hair, dyed it orange, and hitched her wagon to Reykjavík's punk boom. It was a significant choice. From Patti Smith to Siouxsie Sioux to X-Ray Spex to X, punk rock has offered females liberation from the usual beauty standards and aesthetic pieties, a liberation Björk has clung to and demanded throughout her career, even when playing with string orchestras. On the Bravo special, she explains that she became an "art terrorist" because she was "terrified of mediocricy [sic] and narrow-mindedness . . . of small-townness."

Ultimately, even Reykjavík's punk scene provided an inadequate well for this expansive thirst. "In Iceland I was the odd one out; I need to know I'm not the only one."

EPISODE 4

In which our heroine leads an

Icelandic invasion of Europe and

discovers she's an elf

History 101: The world has been shaped by colonialism. Nation-states in every continent were created by European empire builders looking for materials and markets for their burgeoning industrial economies. The world remains divided into countries that were colonizers, and those that were colonies—with the United States holding its special global position partly because it began as the latter and wound up the former. Residents of the European motherland still often look down their noses at residents of their former territories.

In the 1980s, some of the most beautiful guitar-based pop in the world was made by acts from down under such as the Go-Betweens, the Verlaines, and the Chills. But even when those Australian and New Zealand musicians relocated to England, they found themselves disdained by media representatives in the seat of the British Empire—treated like hicks. Björk has cited such colonialist attitudes as a probable source for the conflicts she had with Lars von Trier during the making of *Dancer:* The director is Danish, and Iceland was under Denmark's thumb for more than five centuries.

It was one man's act of unbigoted bravery that saved Björk from being initially swept into the dustbin of not-taken-seriously outsiders. On August 22, 1987, journalist Chris Roberts anointed a record released by the fledgling independent label One Little Indian "Single of the Week" in London's influential *Melody Maker* music weekly. He praised "Birthday," the Sugarcubes' first single, to the high heavens in the sort of self-indulgent purple prose typical of the English music press: "With a dangerously cross-eyed chanteuse who resembles both Denis Lavant and the little girl who *cuts your lips off* in your nightmares, they head straight and bittersweet for the most important things in life. Quite the most astonishing apposite brood of sound (sort of) accompanies these tortured sobs. . . . It breathes, melts, billows, changes shape. Die in the sea with the one you love." If Björk and her band were henceforth treated as exotic oddities ("I could tell everyone that I have four breasts on my back and everybody would believe me because I'm a weirdo from Iceland," Björk was later quoted as saying in *Melody Maker*), at least they were treated as oddities worthy of international attention.

It's fairly rare that a music critic directly affects history; in Roberts's case, he has his own good call to thank. "Birthday" is a delicious lark, an upbeat ballad that crackles and pops with sensual delight. The music—a loping, laid-back beat punctuated with scattered fractals of squonking horns—provides a backdrop for Björk's vocal capers, which escalate from Kate Bush ethereal to an Ethel Merman–esque exclamation: that guttural "brrruoh" belt that has become a Björk trademark but at the time seemed to indicate the sister was from another planet—Iceland indeed. The lyrics are scandalously un-P.C.: about a five-year-old girl's erotic fascination with insects, the earth, and a fifty-year-old man: "they're sucking cigars / he got a chain of flowers / sows a bird in her knickers." Björk has admitted the song is autobiographically based. "I picked on this subject to show that anything can affect you erotically: material, a tree, anything," she told Aston.

"Birthday" brought the Sugarcubes to the public ear, and during their six-year, three-album career, they never left it, scoring numerous hits and *Melody Maker* covers in Europe, becoming a staple of America's nascent modern-rock radio, and touring the United States with U2. They were a fascinating oddball quintet (later a sextet), comprising Björk's ex-husband, the father of her child, Thór Eldon, on guitar; Einar Melax on keyboards, later replaced by Eldon's new wife, Margrét "Magga" Órnolfsdóttir, (on their second and third albums); Bragi Ólafsson on bass; ranting Einar Örn on vocals and trumpet; and Sigtryggur Baldursson on drums. According to *The Rolling Stone Encyclopedia of Rock,* Örn and Ólafsson's was the first openly gay marriage in rock history.

The Sugarcubes had formed out of the ashes of the anarchist punk band Kukl (Icelandic for "witch"), itself a collection of writers and artists. "There was an organization of surrealists who screamed poetry at people and tied catalogs to their foreheads and walked backwards through town," Björk told me. "I fell in love with them; a poet became father of my son. . . . It was punk and literature, with a surrealist sprinkle on it. That was the teenage outburst." The Sugarcubes took themselves somewhat less seriously than Kukl. Their stated goal was to simply be a pop group and spread Bad Taste—the name of their record label and publishing house back home, and their motto. In many ways, the Sugarcubes defined an era in alternative rock: setting up camp (and I mean that in a Susan Sontag way) left of the mainstream pop dial, but preceding the angst and protest of grunge. They were certainly the most famous Icelandic pop stars ever, if not the most famous Icelanders since the sagas were scrawled on animal hides.

Unfortunately, "Birthday" also locked Björk into "elfin woman-child" (to further quote *The Rolling Stone Encyclopedia*) mode, a stereotype with sexist and racist overtones of which she has yet to break free. Repeated media references to her pixieish qualities are in part the fault of lazy, closed-minded journalists who got one idea with one single and have never let go; who patronize Icelanders as if, like their homeland, they're infants who just sprang up from the ocean; who see an Asiatic-looking woman and think "China doll"; who prefer their grown women to be unintimidating and even helpless; who just can't get over their Lolita fantasies.

Björk has not tried terribly hard to dispel the belittling labels. Songs such as "Isobel" and "Hyper-ballad" read like children's stories. In concert, she runs around barefoot. When she thinks, she wrinkles up her nose. She has publicly spoken of fairies and ghosts as real beings. Several of her music videos have been directed by French animator Michel Gondry ("Human Behaviour," "Army of Me") and one by *Ren and Stimpy* creator John Kricfalusi ("I Miss You"); in them, she has hobnobbed with claymation figures or literally been a cartoon character.

"Human Behaviour," her first post-Sugarcubes single and award-winning video, brought Björk to the public eye. In it, a giant teddy bear walks through a magic forest tracking a hunter. (Bears and hunters are recurring themes in Björk videos. "I identify with polar bears," she told *Interview*. "They're very cuddly and cute and quite calm, but if they meet you they can be very strong.") Björk cavorts with *Rudolph*-esque animals while sporting glittering stones like tears under each eye and sleeves that hang down past her fingers as if she's got Daddy's shirt on. It's a video equally at place on MTV, where it was aired regularly, and Nickelodeon.

On songs such as "Birthday" and videos such as "Human Behaviour," Björk seems to be eternally reliving her early, formative years, as if it was an era she hasn't quite resolved—and maybe doesn't want to. "Because *my* mother trusted me from an early age, when I was five or so she gave me a key and I took myself off to school, and I did all my homework, and I dressed and fed myself—I became my own mum, very, very early on, and I developed a relationship to myself where I was the mum *and* the child," she told *Rolling Stone.* That relationship remains central to her identity and artistry. It's a gift to be able to remain connected to the way we perceived and felt the world as kids—as long as we don't live there.

To a large degree, young at heart, inside and out, is the way Björk is. Her hands, for instance, are ridiculously small, like a five-year-old's. Her parents never beat the child out of her; it's her unquenched wonder, untamed imagination, and unbridled enthusiasm that power her genius. I want those qualities from artists, from everyone, from myself. I love her cartoon videos; they're part "Peanuts," part adult comics by artists like Kaz and Matt Groening, and completely unlike the usual MTV fare (where, nonetheless, they have been very popular). I like having a pop star I can enjoy with kids.

"When I see my parents fight / I don't want to grow up," American singer and songwriter Tom Waits has sung, speaking actually for his son, but speaking for all of us. Sweethearts baby-talk to each other in part because passionate emotions make us regress to ages when we hadn't been trained to curb our feelings, to tamp our spirits down and shoulder the weight of adult responsibilities. Psychotherapists encourage patients to release their inner children. People who never shoved their child inside themselves are fun, loving, and fun-loving people.

"She's Vegas!" the RZA of the Wu-Tang Clan said of Björk in *Paper* in 1997. The hip-hop group and Björk had recorded a couple songs together that summer. "A lot of people, they scared to be around us sometimes, but Björk just runs around going, 'Ark ark ark!' It's like we from the same motherfuckin' cusp." It's hard not to hear, see, or even read about Björk and not want to run around with her going "Ark ark ark!" She seems like the kind of person you could say, "Right, let's fly to Paris, dance all night, and eat sundaes for breakfast," and she'd say, "Okay!" She's spontaneous, adventurous, free like that. "Freedom is the biggest aphrodisiac," she says in Paul Lester's biography *Björk*. "The good things in life are having a bottle of red wine and a friend of yours all sleeping in the grass or jumping in the ocean." "I'm driving too fast in cars with ecstatic music on," she sings on the 1993 track "Violently Happy." "I'm daring people to jump off roofs with me." I wanna go.

Björk has described her art as "instinct-driven." Working from an emotional, not an intellectual place has always been the starting point for her. When she first began hanging out with Reykjavík's literary crowd, she was the willful teenager constantly arguing that the poets had to create from their hearts, not their heads. This is ultimately her character Selma's lesson in *Dancer,* whispered to her on the gallows by Catherine Deneuve's character: "Listen to your heart." "She's open and also very connected in a really strong way to the power of her intuition," harpist Zeena Parkins says of Björk. "And on top of that she has skills. It's an amazing combination, because often people who have skills are not so connected to that intuitive process."

Björk remains inextricably linked not only to her instinct and intuition, but also to her imagination. Maybe it's the Viking in her, able to convert ordinary events into fairy-tale sagas. In the book *Post,* a collection of interviews with Björk and her collaborators written by her friend Sjón, an Icelandic poet (and frequent Björk lyricist), Björk explained controversial comments she had made regarding the fact that she, like a lot of her compatriots, believes in ghosts and goblins. "Of course it's complete nonsense," she said—others' literal rendering of the feeling that if "you miss someone very, very much, of course he's following you around, and you're gonna see him."

In fact, Björk is following a century-old tradition of artists who believe that reality is not necessarily as plain as the nose on your face. She remembers when Sjón came to her high school and gave a lecture explaining surrealists, such as André Breton and Georges Bataille. "He said, 'If I feel like a train is driving through my head, it is!' " she recalls in *Post.* To Björk, a video such as "Army of Me," in which she drives around in a giant truck that has a mouth for a motor and goes to see a gorilla that's a dentist, is not infantile but simply follows in the Dada tradition, accepting that a metaphor for a feeling can be its own reality. "I love Michel [Gondry] because he's so naturally surrealist," she says in *Post.* "For me true surrealism is that not only have I got five fingers and I'm sitting on a chair, that's fact, but also the way I feel is fact too. . . . 'Army of Me' is so much about me actually learning that I have to defend myself. I have to stand up and fight the fucking gorilla."

—

All this refusal to grow up—if growing up means losing touch with your imagination, your intuition, your heart—is well and good. But sometimes an artist needs to be taken seriously. Especially if she's a woman, an independent woman, trying to make herself heard—sometimes she has to fight the fucking gorilla. To be honest, there are moments when Björk's so cutesy and coy—like when, in videos, she tilts her head just a little too much to the side, as if it were a wobbly balloon—they make me want to pull a Bangkok airport on her. There's a part of me that cheers when (WARNING! ALERT! I'M GIVING AWAY THE MOVIE'S ENDING!) Selma is finally executed in *Dancer in the Dark;* enough of this tiresomely thick (thick glasses, thick accent, thick-headed) martyr character. Give her kid to Catherine Deneuve—now there's a real, grown-up woman!

There are certain equally thick people out there who will be surprised to learn that I, an out-feminist writer, picked Björk as the musical hero I most wanted to write an e-book about. Hey, I put those pigeonholes away, you can too, buddy! Björk is a perfectly wonderful feminist icon. Even if she doesn't want to be. (In pop, women rarely do.)

Björk's relationship to feminism is complicated—so's mine, yours is too, I bet. On the one hand, she has dismissed the protest politics of early-nineties punk feminists; while the band Bikini Kill was shouting "Suck my left one" at would-be child moles-ters, "Birthday" girl Björk was singing about a "Chihuahua" (the title of a 1992 Sugarcubes song; to be fair, another song on that album is titled "Hetero Scum"). "If the Riot Grrrls had been born in the '30s or '50s, then they could moan and whine," she's quoted as saying in *Björkgraphy*. "But thanks to all the brilliant feminists of this century—writers, artists, and politicians who've said, 'No, we don't want to live in this cage'—the cage has been removed. Now it's time to prove yourself."

This is classic postfeminist balderdash, a belief that an improvement in choices and conditions for some means equality has been achieved for all, and that therefore women should stop their complaining—or, as the band Le Tigre called a song on their 2001 EP, "They Want Us to Make a Symphony out of the

Sound of Women Swallowing Their Own Tongues." Such blithe ignorance is the sure sign of a privileged upbringing. One look at the comparative wages of men and women around the world proves the cage is very much in place.

Of course, being from Iceland, Björk has been more privileged than most modern women. Iceland's equivalent to the United States's Uncle Sam and England's John Bull is the supernatural Woman of the Mountains. In 1980, Icelanders elected Vígdís Finnbogadóttir president, making her the world's first democratically elected female head of state, a post she held for sixteen years. The country also boasted the world's first parliamentary party devoted to feminism, the housewife-driven Women's Alliance. In her own life, Björk has been fortunate to have experienced little discrimination. "I am things numbered one, two, three, four, five, six, down to number fifty and then, yes, I happen to be a woman," she told *Fresh and Tasty* magazine in 1997.

She is, actually, aware that all things are not quite equal. "I think the difference between how men and women are treated is that men are allowed to be characters," she went on to tell *Fresh and Tasty*. "You get the funny guy, the sexy guy, the caring guy, the professor, and all sorts of different characters. But women are just supposed to be 'female.' "

Björk's second video, in fact, was very much about being a female, in a captivating way. For "Venus as a Boy," director Sophie Muller presented Björk as a housewife in a kitchen, musing erotically about this wonderful, strange guy: "He believes in beauty!" She rolls an egg around, then fries it (a scene inspired by one of Björk's favorite books, Bataille's scandalous *Story of the Eye*). Desirous, hungry, and in control, Björk seems like a kid only in that way we all do when we are smitten and daydreaming. The video lovingly captures a moment of everyday magic; it's Björk's contribution to the Women's Alliance.

Björk supports women's rights. "Feminism shouldn't be about making things more difficult, it should be about the *other* thing," she says in *Björkgraphy.* "I believe in a more positive approach, not whining." In other words, she's quick to distance herself from what writer Naomi Wolf has called victim feminism. Perhaps too quick. After all, the Riot Grrrls she criticizes weren't whining; they were growling and shouting, spitting and snotting, like Björk used to do. Emerging from the backlash of the Reagan years in a country where there was no Women's Alliance, American artists such as Babes in Toyland, Bratmobile, L7, and Hole were venting a much-needed anger. Provocative, experimental, giddy, passionate, brave, reckless, sweet, funny, smart, and touching—Björk's work with the Sugarcubes and as a solo artist in the mid-nineties was all of those things, but it rarely raged.

Melody Maker's Chris Roberts noticed this deficiency: *Debut,* her 1993 solo album, made "a mere nightclubber of her guileless sealclubber," England's original Sugarcubes fan complained. Let's be honest: Even when Björk's ripping up teddy bears and wearing a straitjacket, as she does in the video for "Violently Happy," the lady looks wacky and fashionable—and ever so nonthreatening.

When an artist creates, she tries different things, and part of the art-making process is deciding what works and what doesn't. "Listen to your heart" is wonderful advice, assuming your heart's a good communicator. I know mine has led me smack-dab into some bruising relationships and unhealthy situations. If you're in a collaborative medium—and Björk prefers making music with other people—those people may influence your decision; it's hard to hear your heart when you're listening to other hearts too, trying to synchronize pulses. I suspect sometimes Björk has gotten encouraged down paths that were in retrospect poor decisions: her precociousness and preciousness encouraged, like they are in so many girls. Women baby-talk not only to coo love but to get our way, because people don't like the sound of a woman making demands (it's "shrill," "hysterical," "unladylike"). Not that anyone but Björk is to blame for her teddy bear affection.

Björk has certainly done more than her part to expand the repertoire of characters available to women. But there was something missing.

EPISODE 5

In which our heroine fights the

gorilla and proves the

impossible really exists

*H*omogenic is not what one would normally call an aggressive-sounding album. *Atmospheric* is a more appropriate term. With a select palette—strings, vocals, and electronic sounds—Björk and coproducer Mark Bell paint a stark, beautiful, intense soundscape. Yet within the disc's tableau of emotional states are some distinctly pugilistic barbs; gorillas beware. "You think you're denying me of something / well, I've got plenty / you're the one who's missing out," Björk jabs with the opening lines of "5 Years." The song's a challenge to an ex-lover (conceivably British drum 'n' bass pioneer Goldie, to whom she had been engaged). It's the song Sarah Jessica Parker's character on *Sex in the City* should have played when Mr. Big dumped her; I wanted to send a tape of it to my ex-husband, with the lines "I'm so bored of cowards / who say what they want / then they can't handle / can't handle love" recorded extra loud.

The music is almost sarcastically slap-happy, beep, burp, and blipping along, as if out to prove that no coward is going to get Björk down. She sounds ecstatic as she sings the chorus in her throat-clearing belt, like she's working up an extra juicy gob of spit: "I d-a-a-a-re you!" (Ironically, that line mimics the opening song on Bikini Kill's first record, "Double Dare Ya." Bikini Kill were singing to their girlfriends, Björk was singing to a boyfriend. *Vive la différence.*)

In 1996, Björk hit a wall. A number of specific events precipitated the "crash" or "kick," as she alternately called it when we spoke: the Bangkok incident, a club fight between Tricky and Goldie, a letter bomb from a fan who committed suicide. Even without those catalysts, a breakdown may have been inevitable. "I'd been living very fast for four years," Björk told me. "I knew when I left Iceland I wanted to go on a mission. I was ready for it. I wanted danger, and I got it. And it was very satisfying. And then last autumn I had my kick. Sometimes you've got all these things inside you and you don't get them out unless you have stimulation from outside. And sometimes that stimulation has to be quite aggressive.

"It's like Bruce Willis in *Die Hard:* You've got these buildings falling on your head and three children being killed, and that's when what you really are about comes out. I wanted that stimulation, which is a mild word. But you can only do that for so long, and then there's stagnation. And then the biggest challenge is to sit still. . . . And if I could do that for ten minutes—which was, believe me, very hard after four years of five thousand miles per hour—then the big things start coming out."

—

In 1992, the Sugarcubes broke up and Björk became a solo artist. For many of her fans, this was a relief. The Sugarcubes were often too smart for their own good. They wanted to be a pop band, but they wanted it in a patronizing way—pop fans don't necessarily like to be accused of having Bad Taste. Accordingly they often came across as pretentious. And because these "serious" artists and writers didn't always take their music seriously, they also came across as a novelty act. Most irritating to many was the way Einar Örn's amelodic spoken-word bits would run roughshod over Björk's actual vocal talent. I found the Sugarcubes most irritating rhythmically; they made the same error many avant-rockers have made, mistaking busy-ness for complexity. Björk has said that she felt, for her, the Sugarcubes were a dialogue with drummer Siggi Baldursson, and that the two of them had run out of things to say to each other.

Always intended as a lark, the Sugarcubes were never going to be the be-all and end-all for Björk. She began her career at age eleven as a solo artist, after all; that debut album went gold in Iceland. She could have continued in child-prodigy mode, been a teenybop star, but "I didn't want to do another album," she told me. "I didn't want to work with grown-ups, I wanted to work with people my own age. I felt very isolated and uncomfortable with people coming up to me on the street. So I started a punk band when I was twelve; everyone was equal. That's partly why it took me sixteen years to be ready to do my record. . . . I've worked with a lot of brilliant people who have taught me things."

In 1990, Björk satisfied the hankering for jazz she had developed as a kid listening to her grandparents' records. On a break from the Sugarcubes, she recorded an album with Icelandic jazz group Trio Gudmundar Ingólfssonar, named after its pianist, Gudmundar Ingólfsson, who died of cancer the following year. *Gling-Gló* (Icelandic for "ding-dong") is a collection of Icelandic swing classics (yes, there are such things), along with three American golden oldies (by Rodgers and Hammerstein, Hammerstein and Kern, and Leiber and Stoller). The album was a huge hit with the folks back home, and unlike her first album, is still in print and easy to find.

Gling-Gló made it clear that Björk isn't the usual rock 'n' roll singer: Her influences go way back, and all over the place. "My parents listened to a lot of Janis Joplin and Jimi Hendrix, thinking that was the real deal and the rest was crap," she told me. "And at the classical music school, they thought that was great and the rest was crap. And going to my grandparents, and them thinking that was great and the rest was crap. And me coming in like a prankster and throwing a spanner into things: playing Hendrix for my grandparents, or Ella Fitzgerald for the classical people."

Björk was the world's first postrock star. *Postrock* is the term critic Simon Reynolds has popularized to describe acts more influenced by electronic, dub, rap, and dance music than by Elvis and Dylan. Rock 'n' roll belongs to a previous era; Björk can barely stomach the stuff. Explicitly rebelling against her parents, she speaks for a generation that's sick of baby-boom hegemony. Coming from a country whose first major issue as a sovereign nation was whether to expel an American military base from its soil, she also speaks for a world sick of the cultural imperialism represented by American rock 'n' roll. She can be quite withering on the subject:

"I went to the States last January and did loads of interviews," she told me. "They kept saying, 'Electronic music is the next big thing.' And I was like, 'What? They've been making electronic music for fifty years now. Sorry, what do you mean when you say "electronica"?' And they'd say, 'Kraftwerk, and Prodigy, or Massive Attack, or Moby.' I'd just look at them and say, 'I don't get it. As far as I'm concerned, you're talking four different brands of music there, and it's just because they don't have guitarists.' Most people in Europe are brought up on Kraftwerk and Eno. . . . I understand that each country has got a heart, and that guitar is maybe the heart of America. But what annoys me is when they look at anything else as being weird—especially when it's been going on for fifty years. I think we're talking about mediocrity and narrow-mindedness there, which are my greatest enemies. So yes, it does get me defensive.

"All civilizations have got their high point," she continued. "The Japanese had a really good thing going on in the sixteen hundreds. Egypt, we all think pharaohs and Cleopatra. . . . Of course when you have a climax, just like everybody has—you have a good party going on and you're feeling at your best, you're in love or whatever it is that makes you feel you just couldn't feel better—of course you want that to last forever, you want to freeze-frame that. Whatever came with that, whether you were wearing a green jumper or you were living in [a particular] neighborhood, you cling to it. I think that's very human. . . . With the States, obviously the climax was the nineteen fifties, when they still believed in plastic and nylon and Ken and Barbie and products and shopping, and rock 'n' roll was the sound. Of course they want to stay there. They don't want some geezers with synthesizers to come around. . . .

"The American rock 'n' roll industry is more conservative than the electricians' union in Iceland. . . . My father runs the union, so I know that you have to adapt. There's new equipment every fucking year. Once you've learned to be an electrician you have to go to courses just to keep in touch. And everybody in the world is doing that except the U.S. rock 'n' roll industry. They're just staying in their jeans and their black motorcycle jackets and listening to guitar solos."

Grrrilla!

—

Björk did give rock 'n' roll a chance. When she began spending time in London, she checked out the live-music circuit. Not many bands toured Iceland, after all, and she was thirsty to soak up the glories of gigging. She was sorely disappointed with what she heard. "When I started touring with the Sugarcubes, I was really excited about seeing gigs because I'd only seen three concerts in my life," she told me. "It was really exciting to go abroad, music being my obsession and me being twenty years old. And it was black and white: there was absolutely no creativity in rock venues, it was like moldy with cobwebs all over it."

Instead, Björk hit the dance clubs. There, in London's burgeoning electronic scene, where acid house, techno, trip-hop, and drum 'n' bass were all the rave, she found the talent and stimulus she'd been looking for. "I started going clubbing and I realized that the DJs in the cellars, once they get going—and sometimes you have to wait until five or six in the morning—but once they stop pleasing the crowds and play for themselves, they would take off. You just know the difference between magic and not magic. There was something in the air: That sort of full need to be alive, that's where it was happening." She likens the creativity in the clubs to bebop in the forties. "There's nothing like being a fly on the wall when a new music is in the making."

Like many dreamers who grew up in isolated regions, Björk was discovering the real-life thrill of bright lights, big city— everything's great when you're downtown. "I'm addicted to action," she told *Melody Maker* in 1991. She moved to London in 1992. Coming from a place where everyone knows her (and having had a hit record at age eleven, *everyone* knows her), the anonymity of the city was a great relief. City people (except for that asshole Rudy Giuliani) don't look down on pleasure, or difference; a person is free to be whoever or whatever they want to be, to enjoy *la dolce vita*. That's why independent women and gay men flock to urban areas; we're far less likely to end up playing some phony, loveless role, or lying dead in a cornfield. On the dance floor, which in the best clubs is a true melting pot of sex, race, and class, no one judges one another for having a good time—having a good time is the point. "I'm a future woman / in an irresistible world," Björk sang on the Sugarcubes track "Speed Is the Key."

Incredibly turned on by these new club sounds, Björk began writing songs that weren't appropriate for a band setup like the Sugarcubes. She sent a couple to Graham Massey of the hit-making electronic act 808 State, and a musical love affair was born. She sang on two songs on their 1991 album *Ex:El,* and he cowrote two on 1995's *Post.* For years, they made mix tapes for each other of their favorite music. Her song "Headphones" is about falling asleep to one of those tapes; it expresses how profoundly music can affect a person—"Sounds go through the muscles / these abstract wordless movements"—how it can even save a life.

So it was scarcely surprising that for her post-Sugarcubes work, Björk hooked up with geezers with synthesizers.

Björk's early albums are brilliant. I was a Janie-come-lately because of my own critical failure, not hers. Not that I disliked *Debut, Post,* and *Telegram* (a collection of remixes of songs on *Post*); I just didn't pay them much attention. At the time, I needed the outrage purge provided by punk and rap more than the bliss of these fantastic (as in fantasy-filled) dance grooves and love songs. I thought she was a fun weirdo, but the baby act put me off. Besides, being an American, I was more interested in girls with guitars. I still, generally, am; I see a woman wielding an ax as a grab for power, not an acquiescence. I like women who do just that: wield guitars, not strum them passively, like some hippie-chick cliché. On that, Björk and I agree.

What I failed to appreciate was that by eschewing guitars for samplers, Björk was in many ways being the most radical girl of all. Probably even she would admit that women have not caught up with men when it comes to command of technology, largely because we're still not given the necessary hands-on access. This is as true in music as in rocket-building and computers; there are pitifully few female engineers, sound mixers, DJs, and producers. In dance music in particular, women have been relegated to front-person, songbird duties, while men take on the more powerful, and lucrative, writing, programming, and producing roles. A 1997 article in *Spin* on the twenty-two top American "electronica" (a term coined by a man) artists included no women; the article appeared one month after the magazine's special "Girl Issue."

Björk was a truly singular pioneer. At the time, I didn't realize how involved she was with the creation of her music; I mistook her for just a particularly intense diva. In fact, she was producing tracks even on *Debut*. "She's very much taken a producer role with her music," Graham Massey says in the book *Post*. "She's not one of those passive singers who has everything done for her. She's involved in every aspect of the music-making process."

Maybe it's the influence of her electrician father. "I always listened to electronic music, since I was a teenager," she told me. "I discovered Stockhausen when I was eleven or twelve. And then of course I did what everybody did: listened to Kraftwerk and Eno. Then I played synthesizers, did electronic music and stuff."

Or maybe it's because she grew up outside of any one tradition, able to hear, appreciate, and work with almost all of them. She loves harp as much as drum programming. She has a fantastic ear, music-school training, and an insatiable curiosity. I can't imagine another pop star who could work with Scottish percussionist Evelyn Glennie, jazz legend Oliver Lake of the World Saxophone Quartet, Brazilian orchestrator Eumir Deodato, British bhangra star Talvin Singh, American jazz harpist Corky

Hale, new classicists the Brodsky Quartet, new-music composer Hector Zazou, goth girl guitarist PJ Harvey, rappers Wu-Tang Clan and Mike D of the Beastie Boys, hard rockers Skunk Anansie, trip-hop dark star Tricky, and the leading lights of the electronic vanguard: LFO, 808 State, Howie B, Dillinja—not to mention Madonna. Including the numerous people who have remixed Björk singles, the list goes on.

Björk loves to collaborate. "My passion has always been more making music, rather than singing, or doing interviews," she told me. "Since I was in music school, my most exciting thing was co-operating with people. It's just a question of afterwards figuring out who did what." I'm sure her slow road to total artistic independence—*Vespertine* is the first on which she is the sole producer—is in part a result of her insecurity. But mostly, I think she just prefers the spark created by two minds rubbing together. "I could easily have done an album on my own ages ago and done everything myself, but that's not really an ambition for me," she says in *Björkgraphy*. "It was always more challenging to work with other people as different to you as possible, so you can learn from them."

Her collaborators speak glowingly of Björk. "She poured ideas into my head and stirred them around," Michel Gondry says in *Post*. Evelyn Glennie praises "Björk's complete openness to ideas and things, the way she's ready to try absolutely anything and see what comes out of the experiment." For Zeena Parkins, a veteran of New York's experimental music scene, who has played with talents from Marc Ribot to Hole to William Parker, recording *Vespertine* with Björk was a revelatory experience. "She was so open to me doing layers of harp, it was so supportive," Parkins told me. "It didn't feel like something foreign; it felt like I'm hiring you to do what you do, so do it, and do more of it. She was definitely bringing out the inner pretty harp in me—I hate to admit that it's there. That doesn't reveal itself very often, but she was yanking it out of me."

"I'm an umbrella covering dozens of duets, being turned on by a selection of fertile minds, proving 1 + 1 is three," Björk says in the book *Post*.

Her first main partner in crime was Nellee Hooper, who produced and cowrote most of *Debut* and *Post*. Hooper had been in the groundbreaking Bristol sound system the Wild Bunch (out of which came Massive Attack, Tricky, and Portishead) and the massively successful dub-funk group Soul II Soul. He had also coproduced Sinéad O'Connor's number-one single "Nothing Compares 2 U." The king of smooth, Hooper was able to make sense of Björk's overflow of ideas—to make a cohesive album, 1993's *Debut,* out of tracks that venture from the bossa nova–based synth pop of "Human Behaviour" to the whimsical ballad "Venus as a Boy" to the techno-tripping "There's More to Life than This" (recorded in the bathroom of a bar) to the harp-and-vocals cover of the Chet Baker hit "Like Someone in Love." It's a dazzlingly ambitious album that was so successful, Madonna got Hooper to do her next album for her (and Björk to write her the song "Bedtime Story").

1995's *Post* presents more of the different: the blitzkrieg bop of "Army of Me," the fantasia of "The Modern Things," another old cover, this time the big-band "It's Oh So Quiet." This is sincere postmodern bricolage. When the stringed melancholy of "You've Been Flirting Again" streams into the torrid fairy tale "Isobel"—it's a goose-bump moment. Björk relied less on Hooper on *Post,* bringing in Massey and Tricky on some tracks. She was moving out on her own again, with Hooper there as a safety net, as she explained on one track, asking the producer to "Cover Me": "I'm going to prove the impossible really exists."

Björk may not be, and probably doesn't want to be, a household name. But in Europe, and parts of the rest of the world, her first albums made her a bona fide star. She won Britain's Brit Award for Best International Female Artist in 1994, 1995, and 1996, beating, for instance, Madonna. With her forward fashion sense—wearing avant-garde designs by Junya Watanabe, Alexander McQueen, Martin Margiela, and Hussein Chalayan—she was also a style icon, named by *The Face* magazine number nineteen of "The 100 Most Influential People in Fashion." Women all over the world began tying their hair in little knots on top of their heads, à la Björk.

Fame, obviously, has its price. For one, it makes you (un)fair game for vicious gossip, spread to millions courtesy of the tabloid press. Björk was having fascinating romantic as well as artistic collaborations: English DJ Dom T, French fashion photographer Stéphane Sednaoui, Tricky, Goldie, Howie B—not all at once, mind you (though maybe closer in a row than some of her paramours would have liked). She is, quite admittedly, a bit of a sex fiend; she told *Interview* magazine that life, death, and sex are her three obsessions. She confessed to Sylvia Patterson of *Sky* that she's "outrageously sexually greedy" and masturbates every day. One of the hottest Björk items on eBay is a gorgeous black-and-white poster of her naked with three giant, strategically placed leaves. This direct eroticism is part of what gives her girlie act teeth, makes her beguiling instead of cutesy.

And it drives men crazy. Two events happened in the fall of 1996 that made Björk the center of unwanted media attention. A fan in Florida, upset that Björk was engaged to a black man (Goldie), sent her a letter bomb that was intercepted by the post office; the fan committed suicide. Then, at a nightclub in New York, Tricky—also, I surmise, upset that Björk was engaged to Goldie—got into a brawl with the latter, in front of Björk.

The incident that the tabloids positively feasted on, though, had already happened: On February 19, 1996, Björk made her first tour of Asia. Arriving jet-lagged and exhausted at the Bangkok airport, she was greeted by nine television crews. "I didn't realize what a big deal it is in Asia for a western pop act to come there," she told me. "They were having mass hysteria. I always have a really strict line about privacy. When you know you're going to meet a photographer, you put on that coat."

She definitely didn't have her coat on. Footage of her arrival shows Björk looking unwashed and exhausted, her head down and her features set, almost as if she were under attack. She had already said she didn't want to do any interviews. "This woman kept going live on the air, even though we didn't say yes. She kept saying, 'Oh, Björk obviously doesn't have any time for us and is thinking about other things'—she was being quite bitchy. And then she went to my son, live in front of millions, and said, 'How does it feel like? Isn't it terrible to have a pop-star mom who's so full of herself?' I just lost it. I'm not going to one minute say what I did was right. But it was the third time in my life I lost it: Once when I was six, and once when I was seventeen. I just saw red."

Björk attacked the reporter, knocking her down and banging her head on the floor. (Grrrilla!) The attack was aired live, subsequently rebroadcast around the world, and captured in photographs. "Afterwards, when I calmed down, the first thing I did was go to Sindri and say, 'I'm so sorry.' He's never seen me like this. I explained to him, 'When so-and-so took your car and lost it, that's how I felt. Do you understand? I'm so sorry.' He just looked at me and said, 'No, Mum, don't worry, I understand. What I don't understand is why didn't you hit the guy with the camera first, and then go for the reporter. Mum, next time, *think.*' Now when I go out and people ask for autographs and stuff, he walks in front of me and says, 'Don't interrupt her.' That's weird when you've got somebody you've protected all your life suddenly stand up and start protecting you." Who was walking whom across the street now?

Suddenly the self-declared "down-to-earth" artisan was an internationally embarrassed diva. It was time for the future woman to take stock. "There are things that are great, and then a few years later, maybe that's not what you need, and then a few years later, you need them again. Sometimes speed is really good for you, and sometimes it's crap. We want it like that. We want these eighty or however many years we get to live to be very colorful and diverse. Somewhere along the line I made a wish unconsciously to take as fully part of things as I could, and that means you've got to be ready to end periods and start new ones. And change. And of course it's painful. But when you plant a wish like that, that you want to experience and feel maximum, you've got to realize what comes with it."

EPISODE 6

In which our heroine discovers

there's no place like home, and

the narrator discovers our

heroine

B jörk did not strike me as an elf.

We met at my hotel in Reykjavík. She showed up quite late. The hotel staff was excited she was going to be there, and re-assuring while the photographer, Cherry Kim, and I waited—as if feeling protective of their slightly naughty national treasure. A tardy celebrity was scarcely something new to us, but we were a little worried, as our time with Björk was limited. She arrived, fi-nally, not really apologizing—what's the point?—but ready to do business.

Her Björkness and I headed off alone to a nearby coffee shop, Caffe Mokka, for an hour of interview. She was very serious, leaning carefully into the mike to make herself heard over the cappuccino machine, to ensure her words would not be missed or misunderstood. Her unusual accent certainly contributes to her quirky rep: she has the occasional non-native English speaker's odd choice of words, she rolls her *R*s deliciously, and her speech, like her music, has a cadence all its Icelandic own. But I did not feel like I was speaking to a child. Actually, although I'm one year older than Björk, I felt intimidated, like I was conversing with someone far more worldly and experienced than myself, in a way that not every rock star impresses me. This was not the "elfin woman-child" I expected to meet.

Male music journalists often impugn the objectivity of their female peers; they think we fall for every Lothario with a cucumber in his pants whom we get the chance to meet. But it's my belief that it's the boys that slip in their drool more often. After all, they don't get to interview members of the opposite sex regularly; "women in rock" is a recent and fleeting fad, and female artists traditionally get short shrift in the rock press (see the anthology I edited with Ann Powers, *Rock She Wrote: Women Write About Rock, Pop, and Rap,* for more on this subject). Many men, certainly the differently socialized ones who tend to become rock critics, can't talk to a pretty girl without visions of sugarplums dancing in their heads. In proportion to our numbers in the field, I can think of more male critics who have famously bedded, wedded, or tried to bed and wed female stars than I can vice versa (Cameron Crowe and Nancy Wilson, Legs McNeil and Sinéad O'Connor, Bart Bull and Michelle Shocked).

Every interview is a seduction, or a standoff. Most stick to intellectual tangos. In general—and I'm obviously making generalizations here that vary for every person and situation—there's a different dynamic when it's a woman interviewing a woman. We draw different quotes and behavior, and receive different impressions. After reading a drove of past articles about the Pretenders, I once walked into a hotel suite to interview Chrissie Hynde, expecting her to kick my ass, but instead we drank tea and giggled.

As Björk once told *Rolling Stone,* her reputation is only half-true: "People see the kid in me: they think I'm innocent and naïve and all those things, but being organized and hardworking is completely second nature to me." She came across as serious to me because, while I like a laugh at least as much as the next person, I was prepared to take her seriously.

That's part of the story, at least. The other part is that at the time I met her, in the year after her crash, Björk had started taking herself more seriously.

After a bomb had nearly been delivered to her home, Björk left London. That phase of her life was over. "You just want to go and never come back," she explained to Bravo, still sounding shell-shocked. Besides, she missed the ocean. She wound up at a friend's studio in the south of Spain, where she recorded most of *Homogenic*. The Bravo profile shows Björk walking on the beach with her headphones on. "I went to Spain to record one song. And then I walked in there and said, 'That's it, I'm staying,' " she told me. "There was so much nature there; it's very raw."

Ironically, the "hom" of *Homogenic* is Iceland; one of Björk's goals was to sonically represent her birthplace. Her musicologist friend Asmundur Jansson prepared a history of Icelandic music for her prior to recording. "I want to be truthful about Iceland, and being from Iceland—and I don't mean Viking helmets and all of that shit," she said. But she didn't want to work there—there were too many distractions, too many friends and family to see, parties to attend. "If I'd come back here, I would have gone back to my old mates. I needed no one."

Björk's new seriousness of purpose is evident on *Homogenic*. With its orchestral arrangements and themes of loss and learning, this is adult listening. Björk had obviously had a bit of a self-reckoning. The anger expressed on "5 Years" was aimed inward as well as out. "How could I be so immature / to think he would replace / the missing elements in me?" she sang on "Immature."

"Thought I could organize freedom / how Scandinavian of me," she sang derisively, and hilariously, on "Hunter."

Björk wasn't just beating up her inner gorilla. She was having an emotional and artistic breakthrough, learning to listen to and voice her heart. "I wanted to be able to say [the album] was mine, to be more truthful about what I'm about, who I am," she said to me. "I've got fifty years to go, and I'm just slowly getting closer to what I'm about. I think we all are.

"For me this album was going back to basics. On *Debut* and *Post*, all the songs were written over a long period, but all the arrangements were done in England, over a period of four years, where I visited a lot of things, and got introduced to a lot of exciting things, and I was giving nine thousand and accepting nine thousand. I knew it would take two albums to get rid of that back catalog. That's why I called them *Debut* and *Post*, before and after. Now it's time to come back to where I'm from. When I say that, I mean maybe more musically than geographically. Back home, whatever that means.

"I decided to start from the beginning and cut all the crap, because it's very easy to keep people's attention with nine thousand different toys. I went down to saying, 'What are the three toys that are the most important when it comes to noise?' I would say the voice, because we're all experts in the human voice. We can pick up the phone with a complete stranger, and they could say this, but we'd know they meant that. And strings have always had a really good impact on me. I was wondering why that is, because I'm so fond of new things, and strings have been around for ages. I think there must be something very similar in strings to our nerve system. You've got a network of nerves, and when you feel, I think a nerve does something similar to a violin string—a violin is like the audio version of a nerve. Because everybody, when you see a film and hear a string, you go *ooh ooh ooh.*

"I think the voice celebrates the oxygen, and that's one network in our bodies. The strings, the nerves, are another. And the beat is the pulse, which is the blood, the heart. The pulse is . . . you've got a happy song, and that's a hundred and twenty beats per minute, the same way we feel when we're happy. An aggressive song is a hundred and sixty bpm, like drum 'n' bass. And when you want to chill out, you go down to sixty bpm.

"Even though it looks like I've got it all thought out, these are just games. I don't work that strictly by a formula. But it's nice to play around."

Nellee Hooper was gone; her new primary cohort was coproducer Mark Bell, of Black Dog Productions and LFO. "I had a pretty clear vision, but Mark Bell just naturally—we didn't plan it—but he became a big part of the album. I knew what I wanted. I described it to several people but they didn't get me, which I don't blame them: Sometimes the descriptions are pretty blurred. Mark sort of functioned like a safety net for me. He would sit there, and I would run around in this emotional roller coaster and do nine thousand things and look at him and see if they were okay or not. I really trust him. I've listened to his music for seven years, really fiercely. We call each other up quite often, if I want to have a conversation with someone about technical things that would drive other people nuts." Just a couple of nerds in love with music.

Björk says she works intuitively, that she's an emotional roller-coaster, but I suspect those are male dismissals of her smarts that she has internalized. In fact, *Homogenic* was fascinatingly thought out, conceptualized from the get-go. "This album, like all things, I started off saying, 'Okay, it's time to do something completely different now.' You set your target to there; it's very important to have a target. Of course, you're human, and things develop, take their own forms and shapes—you've got to let them do that. But the first target was string arrangements and beats, and that was it. I was going to be really military about the fact there'd be no bass line, no other instruments; I was going to have the voice in the middle, the beats on the right, and the strings on the left. And by using the balance button, any person with headphones or stereo could decide if they just wanted to hear the strings and the voice, or if they just wanted to hear the beats and the voice."

Great idea, as any headphones geek will attest: two albums in one, one retro, one techno. But the final forms and shapes were even better. Instead of dividing them up, Björk and Bell layered and entwined the three networks (strings, voice, and beats) and added keyboards, bass, accordion, horns, and harmonica—but no guitar—creating organic, living wholes. Collectively, these are her most fully realized songs. "I've always been very fierce about structure," Björk said. "When it comes to chord and song structure, I'm like—lethal's not the right word—I'm very, very disciplined. . . . I've had people say they think I'm free-forming through the whole album, and I'm definitely not. Even the remixes, I'm very strict—that's the word I was looking for before—about structure." The lady doesn't just spew and coo.

In this less cacophonous environment, Björk's voice stretches and unfolds in ways only hinted at on her previous albums. "Unravel" (written and produced by Björk and longtime keyboard accompanist Guy Sigsworth) begins with her just singing "duh duh" and breathing, but worlds are contained within the nuances she gets out of those nonsense syllables. Once she starts singing the words—"while you are away / my heart comes undone"—you're on the edge of your seat, soaking in this diva's private love confessional, delivered in cascades. And then follows the dramatic, act-closing climax of "Bachelorette," a tour-de-force symphony of strings, singing, and a flamenco beat. Curtains. Act Two.

Björk confirmed that improved confidence powered her voice on *Homogenic*. "When I was in the Sugarcubes, I was only one sixth of the band; I wasn't responsible for keeping the structure of the song," she told me. "When I started doing my own records, because my biggest experience was with singing, that was where I felt secure. But in things like songwriting and arrangements, I didn't have the same confidence, so my voice was the skeleton. It was the boring old matrix not doing anything adventurous, just staying in one place, to keep the song together. Then I could experiment with the other things. And now I feel more comfortable with songwriting and the other things, so my singing voice has gone a bit off duty. It doesn't have to be the one who gets there at nine. This time around, I think I had more freedom."

Homogenic may have sold less than Björk's previous records, but I still believe it's her best. "People have told me it takes a lot of listens to sink in," Björk said modestly. "I think this one is less compromising than the other albums." *Post* and *Debut* are fabulous collections of songs and styles, but they don't cohere like *Homogenic*'s ten tracks. In this digital age, when compact discs—which can hold many more minutes of music than vinyl LPs—overflow with filler, *Homogenic* is a concept album. You can listen to it from start to finish without thinking about pressing SKIP; you *want* to listen to it from start to finish, over and over. If Björk was being reticent about personal matters during our interview, maybe it was because it was all there on disc: the story of a crash, the death represented by "Pluto," and the phoenix's rebirth, in the form of faith in one's feelings: "All Is Full of Love."

"This album is quite different emotionally. *Debut* is quite shy, like a blank page. The second one is like this chick has lived in the arrogant city for a while, she's living large—the rude girl, indulging, having just a bit too good of a time. This one the songs are really under a lot of pressure, like megakilos of pressure, and how do you cope with it. Maybe being a bit heartbroken as well, but still being a bit of a warrior, still believing in love."

No wonder I, heartbroken ex-wife, could relate. "Hunter" is about realizing that it's okay to want more than one love during one's life, to not think that that makes one less of a woman, or human. I'm going hunting . . .

The album's cover is as gorgeous as the music within, but it shows Björk under pressure, not Björk the warrior. Styled by bad-boy designer Alexander McQueen, Björk's the China girl again, wearing an improbably dimensioned silk robe, her hair piled on her head resembling two toadstools, a tall choker like armor encasing her throat. The photograph is by Nick Knight. "The photo shoot was one of the most difficult photo shoots I've ever done. I couldn't move, I was gaffer-taped. I had to express myself through that. And this was my album cover! The photo looks really uncomfortable, and that's the point. It looks like somebody has been put into a very difficult situation. 'The less room you give me, the more space I've got,' " Björk told me, quoting "Alarm Call."

Once again, her music's freedom conflicted with the trap of her image. And Björk was about to face her biggest crisis yet, as she embarked on her most famous and controversial collaboration to date.

EPISODE 7

In which our heroine loses the

battle but wins the war

M y friend Michelle watched *Dancer in the Dark* with her ears.

Lars von Trier filmed *Dancer* [www.dancerinthedark.com] using handheld digital video cameras; the result, especially for the first half-hour, is like a home movie, all shaky and full of quick cuts—a dizzying presentation that nauseated several people I know, as if they were suffering motion sickness. One person at Björk's record label reportedly was rushed to the hospital during a screening. Michelle couldn't stomach the director's visual experiment. So she closed her eyes, and proceeded to enjoy the movie.

Why not watch *Dancer* in the dark? The film, after all, is about a woman who loses her eyesight over the course of the movie. There are two scenes in which Selma's friend Kathy, played by Catherine Deneuve, patiently sits in a theater and explains what's happening on screen to her sightless companion, much to the annoyance of a local patron. Hushed, Kathy grabs Selma's hand

and represents the chorus line's dance by kick-parading her fingers around Selma's delighted palm; that's what friends are for. "To me it was about how we all work with different senses," Björk said at the New York Film Festival press conference. "Me personally, seventy percent of me is very audio driven, about thirty percent maybe, the eyes. So for me it was a chance to speak out for the people [like myself]. It seems that most of the world is driven by the eye, right? We design cities to look great, but it always sounds horrible. We design telephones to look great but sound horrible. I think it's about time the other senses were being celebrated."

Björk designed *Dancer* to sound great. As composer of the film's majestic music, it was crucial for her that someone like Selma, or Michelle, could enjoy it using only this underappreciated sense. When she found out that changes had been made to the soundtrack without her permission during filming, she left the set for a weekend, returning with a manifesto demanding, among other things, absolute control over the film's music.

This confrontation quickly became legendary; there were reports of smashed equipment. Reputedly, for the fourth time in her life, Björk saw red. *Dancer,* loved and hated in the film community, was almost as famous for the friction between Björk and von Trier on-set as for the final product they achieved together. This was a movie whose drama—and import—continued to unfold long after the credits had stopped rolling.

With von Trier, Björk had chosen a collaborator who had his own film vision, not someone willing to have ideas poured into his head. He was not hired to help her bring her goals to reality, as her album producers and videomakers had been. Quite the opposite: As screenwriter and director, von Trier was the film's auteur, Björk the hired help—even if she did lodge a spanner in his works. Confrontation may well have been inevitable. "When two geniuses who are used to being in their own environment and are used to creating their own rules come together, it's not only a love fest, but it's a time when all the energies that can happen come to the foreground," *Dancer* choreographer Vincent Paterson, who plays the insipid director of the local production of *The Sound of Music* in the film, said at the New York press conference. In the touchy-feely language one might expect from the choreographer of *Evita* and Michael Jackson's Bad tour, Paterson blamed the film's creative tension on, originally enough, the absence of an interfering producer figure. "We never had anybody over our shoulder telling us what to do, telling us, 'Okay, you have to change this script, you have to do that.' Consequently what happens is all of that love and anger and everything that you feel as a family is turned towards one another. It hurt my feelings a little bit that this whole thing has turned into a difficult star and a difficult director. This was really a very incredible family situation, and I really feel it was more of a love fest than anything else."

It was, concededly, a longtime love that first led Björk to this risky venture. She had been interested in soundtracks and musicals since an early age; as a kid, she saw *The Sound of Music* twenty times. Her first top 30 single in England, "Play Dead," was written for the film *Young Americans.* Soundtracks were part of the mix that inspired *Debut,* "because they capture lots of different moods," she says in *Björkgraphy.* "It allows human feelings to exist, the music allows you to be unpredictable, whereas pop music today is so clinical and sterile. There's so much bad pop music around because people don't believe in magic anymore." Discussing her future plans at the book's end, Björk says, "I would love to write a modern musical."

A natural saga-teller, Björk has long conjured up in her lyrics stories that beg to be visualized, and she has been prolifically adept at translating her audio imagination into moving images.

More than perhaps any other pop star, she has created videos that are minimusicals, complete with plot lines and stylized sets. Erstwhile skateboard documentarian Spike Jonze (who later directed *Being John Malkovich*) shot "It's Oh So Quiet" as a Busby Berkeley–esque, Technicolor tribute to *The Umbrellas of Cherbourg,* the acclaimed 1964 film by French director Jacques Demy. The video starts in a tire shop, then moves out to the street, where Björk dances with a mailbox, cavorts with a group of women with parasols, then floats up to the sky.

Von Trier has said that it was Spike Jonze's video that first led him to approach Björk about the musical he was writing, itself influenced by *Cherbourg,* which had starred Deneuve. Björk had already tried her hand at acting a couple of times. In 1987 she starred in *The Juniper Tree,* a black-and-white version of a Brothers Grimm fairy tale directed by Nietzchka Keene and set in Iceland. In this rather twee, Gothic movie, far from being blind, Björk's character has supernatural visions—yes, she sees dead people. Björk also had a cameo in the 1994 Robert Altman flick *Ready to Wear* (*Prêt-à-Porter*).

But Björk initially refused to appear in von Trier's film. "At first I was just going to do the music," she said at the New York press conference. Planning to fulfill her modern-musical composing ambitions, she took the screenplay in hand. "I guess after reading the script, I fell in love with this girl. And then feeling what her different emotional states were, being a little bit like satellites swirling around her. And then after a year Lars insists, and I guess I could be stubborn and say no for another ten years, but I'd sort of fallen even more in love with this woman, and felt like defending her."

Defending her? From whom?

The news that Björk and von Trier were filming together sent ripples through the cultural cognoscenti. Von Trier was famous in the film world first for declaring revolt against the filmmaking establishment with his "Vow of Chastity." He and other upstart art filmmakers, dubbing themselves Dogme95 [www.dogme95.dk], released this manifesto, in which they called for a revolt against "the film of illusion," vowing not to use artificial lighting, filters, phony props, and so on. Von Trier then forced the establishment to pay attention to his renegade talent with his 1996 film *Breaking the Waves,* which won the Grand Jury Prize at Cannes and earned star Emily Watson an Oscar nomination. The idea of Björk, a musical rule-breaker, collaborating with this notorious film rebel was tantalizing.

However, von Trier's treatment of his actors, and his heroines, had already raised hackles among many filmgoers. For his film *The Idiots,* he had his cast participate in an orgy. *Breaking the Waves* was an emotionally brutal film wherein Watson's character plays a naïve-to-the-point-of-idiocy, intuitive, trusting, idealistic, and sensual woman (sound familiar?) who, in a fevered and not very believable delusion, thinks she must sacrifice her body to save her ailing husband. On the one hand, the movie was an attack on the ways in which Christianity has historically infantilized and oppressed women, by demanding they be chaste of knowledge. And yet von Trier's beatification of his innocent, imbecilic heroine hardly presents an alternative role model. Her martyrdom is excruciating to watch, even if that is precisely von Trier's point. Besides, the last thing the world would seem to need is another suffering female martyr. [us.imdb.com/Bio?von +Trier,+Lars].

When word of *Dancer* first began circulating, fans of Björk worried that playing a character like Watson's would just perpetuate many of the most common stereotypes about Björk, which the singer had been struggling to refute. In fact, the character of Selma is often disappointing, playing up Björk's worst qualities.

Her passivity (she mainly speaks only when spoken to) and flakiness (she lives in a perpetual daydream) are maddening. On the other hand, like Björk, she is also incredibly hardworking, stubborn, and a dedicated mother.

It's clear from the first seasick half-hour where *Dancer* is headed. As if going blind weren't enough, Selma's an immigrant, a single mother, and a factory worker struggling not only to make ends meet, but also to save money so her son can have the eye surgery that will save him from her fate; can you spell *martyr*? Sure enough, trying to recover the money for the operation from the neighbor who has stolen it (speaking of not very believable plot twists), Selma commits murder and is sentenced to death.

Von Trier may eschew the usual cinematic tricks, but make no mistake, he is the most manipulative of filmmakers. That's because he's interested not in entertaining (god, no!), but in creating an argument rendered as a vision, that will in turn change the way its viewers see the world. In order to make his point, he forces his plot, and the audience's suspension of disbelief, into places you wouldn't think they could go. Watching *Dancer* was one of the most wrenching film experiences I've had, even if, as one video-store clerk/wag dismissed it, you could see the wrenches.

There have been conflicting opinions as to whether Björk can and did act. At the press conference in Cannes, Deneuve said, "She can't act, she can only be." In the press kit for the movie, von Trier says, "she gives an incredible performance and it's not acted, it's felt." Björk swallows this line of thinking. "I think I'm very innocent as an artist," she said in New York. "As experienced as I am after twenty years of being in studios and being quite a craftsman and academic, or whatever, I'm very naïve and innocent with acting. I guess the only way I could do this was [to] fall in love with this girl and jump off the cliff and everything go wow. It was very instinct-run."

Undoubtedly Björk became extraordinarily immersed in her character. But that's a method of acting; in fact, that's method acting. Björk's portrayal is stunningly refreshing because she doesn't use the usual tricks of the thespian trade. "Being with Björk, who wasn't carrying a lot of this technical baggage with her, was just thrilling for us," costar David Morse said at the New York press conference. "I was surrounded by very experienced people," Björk said. "I kept asking them, 'Is it supposed to be like this? It seems a bit funny.' And they kept convincing me that they would maybe not have done it this way, but everything was absolutely all right."

Selma is not Björk. There are obvious stylized traits Björk developed for the role, such as pushing up her glasses, feeling for objects she can't see, and constantly putting her hand over her mouth as if she were trying to hide a smile—or to not break the rule about being seen and not heard. Selma is a fascinatingly original character because Björk is: The correlation is not an equation, it's an equivalence—one oddball's empathy for another.

With his deeply metaphoric script, his shrewd casting choice, and his unorthodox methods of filming (such as shoving the camera in actors' faces), von Trier creates a genius vehicle for Björk. But *Dancer*'s success is primarily due to the performance she gives. Wearing no makeup, skin broken out, hair greasy, heavy black glasses sliding down her nose—Selma's the homeliest heroine you may ever fall for. Sometimes, her gestures and enthusiasms are so inappropriate, they're painful to watch, and thereby compel your compassion, your desire to protect her, all the more. And then Björk makes this woman's inner world, so different from the hard, dull world around her, come vividly to life, so that it sweeps everything else away . . . at least for the duration of a song.

Her character may be closemouthed, but when she does smile, it's a soliloquy: Her lips turn up slowly at the tips until they've formed a Cheshire crescent; dimples cave in; eyes get not twinkles but rays. That smile's a gateway to everything Selma can't say in her broken English, in her shy awkwardness, her utter introversion mirrored in her growing myopia. Her completeness in this internal world is so amply realized that when her eyesight is finally gone, you don't have any sense her world has diminished. As Björk sings, "I've seen it all / there's no more to see." Who needs to see when there's so much to hear?

Noises—the scratch of a pencil on paper, of a train on the tracks—lead Selma into reveries. Suddenly, the gray, grainy screen turns brightly colored, strings soar, and the world breaks out into song and dance. "The machines make these rhythms, and I start dreaming, and it becomes music," Selma says, in what could be an autobiographical statement by Björk. The way she says "r-r-rhythms" is itself a small miracle: Her face twitches at 160 beats per minute, rippling with delight at the mere utterance of the word. Selma, like Björk, is obsessed with rhythm; she wants there to be drums and tap dancing in the amateur production of *The Sound of Music* she's in. As she lies on a cot waiting to be taken to the gallows, her fingers tap out the beat in her head.

The musical numbers are Selma's world—her *Madame Bovary* and *Sister Carrie*–style daydreams—brought to life. "When we were going through the whole process of making the film," she said in New York, "it became very clear that there was always a question of some fantasy versus reality. The dialogue scenes are reality, the musical scenes are fantasy. That seems to be what this film is sort of about. It's not necessarily a solution, but it's about where do those two things meet."

Actually, it's about where do they part. It's this fantasy world that you can't bear to see vanish when Selma is hanged. Everything else, after all, has already disappeared for her; she's blind, incarcerated, separated from her son. But throughout the life of the film, Björk has created a representation of psychic triumph over adversity, of a character remaining true to herself despite all pressures—a representation that is so winning that even though Selma's execution is inexorably built up to, it's impossible to take.

Impossible, I surmise, for Björk to take also. She was deeply pained by the filmmaking experience, so much so that she subsequently resigned from acting. Although she has offered other reasons and excuses for her differences with von Trier, my theory is she was fighting for Selma's life. She was refusing to accept the passive stoicism of von Trier's character. She had gorillas in her sights. Maybe she actually thought she could change the ending. After all, she had wrought major changes elsewhere, causing the murder scene, for example, to be rewritten. Björk took the role of Selma because she wanted to defend this character for whom she had fallen. At the end of the day, her defense fails.

Or does it?

Dancer is von Trier's airing of the conflict between his childhood fascination with Gene Kelly films and his parents' view of them: "My parents were Communists and they thought that all musicals were American rubbish," he says in the film's press kit. As part of his pointed commentary, von Trier doesn't give us a Hollywood ending. "You will always be there to catch me / when I fall," Selma sings in the ode "In the Musicals." In this musical, no one's there. The rope doesn't break, there's no cowboy on a horse waiting beneath the gallows to ride off into the sunset with a startled, relieved Björk. She dies. This is the death sentence. This is capital punishment in the United States of America, something Denmark—like most civilized countries—doesn't have. I take this to be von Trier's primary point: that the same country that created all these gorgeous, life-affirming musicals is a nation that kills its own people. This is a reality that can't be fantasized away, that remains after the daydreams have been silenced. This also may explain why the film did not storm the American box office: In a year in which George W. Bush became president, a film that portrays executions as terrible tragedies was not going to have great popular appeal. And this is why the film is so important, and why Björk was never going to change its conclusion.

"I'm deeply against the death penalty," von Trier says in the film's press statement. Then he goes on: "On the other hand, execution scenes are God's gift to directors. They're very efficient. If you're going to be a martyr you have to die."

For what is Selma martyred? What cause does she represent that will live beyond her, for which her death will give new life? The fight against capital punishment, perhaps. But I think von Trier's also arguing for a larger cause, one that is, despite his reckless slaughtering of them, very pro-women: that people have the right to be different, to fantasize when they're supposed to be filling factory orders, to be a single mother, to play the lead in the local musical even though "she sings funny and her dancing's not all that great" (as a character says of Selma), to stay alive.

In that case, Björk may have lost the battle but she won the war. In all the drama about the drama, she came across as the heroine, the bright new talent whose flame was being prematurely snuffed out by this notorious Hollywood-bashing director. Her "I'll never act again" declaration at Cannes created a sensation; what had he done to her? By the New York Film Festival several months later, she had softened her tone. "It definitely felt like [being] blindfolded, entering the unknown—the first people to go to Antarctica, that kind of pioneerism," she said of making *Dancer.* "But the experience was like a lot, a lot, a lot of voltage running through you—sometimes quite painful, but that's because of the things that this girl went through, they were not very happy. All in all it's something that you do once in a lifetime, and feel lucky that you could try to feel like this once in your life."

Besides, with her album version of *Dancer,* Björk got to present Selma's story the way she saw—or rather, heard—it.

Selmasongs is not, as the title indicates, precisely the movie's soundtrack. Although dialogue and the sounds of people dancing are included on some cuts, parts of the album have been remixed (Björk again worked with Mark Bell). Actor Peter Stormare is replaced by angel-voiced Thom Yorke of Radiohead on the love-song duet "I've Seen It All." And most significantly, the penultimate song in the movie is nowhere to be found on *Selmasongs.*

Early on in the film, Selma discusses her love of musicals. She explains to Stormare's character that she always likes to leave after the next to last song, so that she doesn't have to witness the end, with all its grand, phony closure. In *Dancer,* "Next to Last Song," as it's identified in the film's credits, is the song Selma sings on the scaffold, in a not-mute protest of being killed, as she makes the real world listen to her world. It is the film's emotional and thematic linchpin: the song that ties all the loose threads together and makes you realize why you've sat through the preceding two hours of painful, beautiful, frustrating, touching art-brut soap opera with giddily brilliant (and dumbly choreographed) musical, Technicolor breaks (picture *Forrest Gump* as filmed by Ingmar Bergman with 1940s Hollywood song and dance). The song narrates—and almost allows you to escape—the riveting, devastating climax. It's the soundtrack of one of the most powerful moments in recent cinematic history, a moment that's all about sound, as Björk, a cappella, sings in that great free voice, "This isn't the last song." Then the floor opens, and her throat closes forever.

The omission of "Next to Last Song" from *Selmasongs* is a major statement by Björk. At the press conference in New York, I asked her why she left this track, as well as Selma's jailhouse rock of "My Favorite Things" (what a single it would have made!), off the album.

Björk's answer: "After I had been shooting the film I was ready to prepare for the soundtrack album. It was [a question of], should I repeat the film and do a CD which is a replica of the film, or should the CD stand in its own right for people that would never have seen the film? I think after thinking about it a little bit, I came to the conclusion that the film should be the film, the CD should be the CD, and the CD being the audio of the film, [it] probably stood for more the fantasy side of Selma. And in Selma's fantasy, as you know, the ones who saw the film, everything's amazing, everything comes through, everything's excellent. This is the place where the songs actually take off and they go into the magical world. So I ended up picking the songs that did that. For the times where Selma in the film made an effort to make that transition into fantasy world but it didn't work out . . . I left these occasions out."

She offered a slightly more succinct explanation to *Premiere* magazine: "I see the album not as the soundtrack to the film but rather as the realization of Selma's dream. I want this record to be my gift to Selma."

It's a gorgeous gift. Björk remakes Hollywood's formulaic ditties in her own wonder-full way. She's more respectful of the medium than red-diaper baby von Trier. Still, this is unlike any musical you've ever heard. Obviously, coming from Björk, it's not a rock musical. It could, in fact, be called the first techno musical. Björk and Bell mix *Homogenic*-style drum 'n' bass atmospherics into the found sounds of feet stomping and machinery clanging. Sometimes the movie noises are replaced by digital analogs; the taps of Joel Grey's feet on "In the Musicals" are electronic buzzes. *Selmasongs* can be a sound-effects record gone operatic.

It is simultaneously deeply sentimental. "Cvalda" is Selma's statement of defiant difference; exclaiming nonsense sounds like a square-dance caller, she entices Kathy to break out of her somber surroundings and dance a little. The song's followed, in timeless fashion, by the Gershwin-worthy, string-drenched duet "I've Seen It All"—Hollywood heroines can't be *too* independent. Even numbers about blindness, and those about death ("Scatterheart" and "107 Steps"), are whimsical flights of fancy. Struggling and moody, the album version of *Dancer in the Dark* is still aiming for the light at the end of the tunnel. It ends with the swelling hopes of "New World." The music's the same as "Next to Last Song," but the lyrics (like all those on the album, written by von Trier and Sjón) are different: "In wonder, I wonder / what happens next / A new day, a new world to see." Strings break through the mist in rays of clarity, and Björk gets her happy ending.

"New World" is the last song of the movie; it plays as the credits roll. But, like the paragraph of text that fills the screen after Selma's execution, it feels tacked on, a Hollywood note of hope appended to von Trier's dark finale. Perhaps it is what von Trier is referring to when, at the end of the interview included in the *Dancer* press kit, he says, "I think that the more I work, the less my own person is involved. If you really work with a character, with an actor, it's as if you were making a documentary. You don't design something, you *investigate* something that is already there. Because it isn't my person and since it isn't only about things that happen in my twisted little brain, perhaps the work becomes more accessible."

Scholars have written about the importance of the male gaze—the fact that films are made for and from men's perspectives—to the shaping of the cinematic experience. *Dancer* may present the triumph of the female listen.

EPILOGUE EPISODE

In which the narrator and our

heroine meet again

In four years, my distant admiration for Björk has snowballed into full-on fandom. Because she has been committed to living her life to the extreme and expressing it without compromise, she's an endlessly rich subject. The more I find out about her, the more she emerges as a real person and a creative artist, the more I like her. I suppose I fell for her like she fell for Selma. Certainly, I want to defend her.

And then there are the affinities, the character traits that, when we find them in celebrities, validate them in ourselves. Like Björk, I'm a small-town girl who had to go to the big city to find freedom, yet I remain deeply connected to the geography that first sculpted me—the Upper Peninsula of Michigan. Like Iceland, it's a harsh, beautiful, remote land, where I've spent summers since I was a kid, where I was camped out in a cabin when I got the *Request* assignment, and where, ultimately, the homogenizing pressures are too oppressive to remain for long. Around the same time of my interview with Björk, art critic Lucy Lippard's book *The Lure of the Local: Senses of Place in a Multi-centered Society* was published; I remember thinking that's what *Homogenic* was expressing and I was discovering: how we modern women can have more than one place like home. We don't need to click our ruby slippers to get there; we carry it with us. Maybe that's what Björk meant by *Vespertine*'s working title: *Domestika.*

After Florence, after Iceland, after Michigan, I cocooned myself in my East Village apartment, redecorating my bedroom to look like the birch forest I had driven through that fall—a vista of white trunks and yellow leaves. Three years later, researching this book, I discovered that *björk* is Icelandic for "birch."

Mainly, Björk and I are "those kind of people" she described to *Flaunt.* Or as she told David Toop in the *Dancer* press kit, "Music is a very introverted thing, very personal and private. Actually I think quite a lot of people who are into music are not very good in social situations. Music is like a rescue thing."

Maybe Selma was martyred so that the filmgoing audience that doesn't follow music could discover Björk. The singer got major mileage out of *Dancer* in markets she had never before reached. For a time in the fall of 2000 she was everywhere, in every daily and weekly newspaper; in film, music, and women's magazines; in *Entertainment Weekly, Newsweek,* and *Time.* She was a slice of human originality at the Golden Globe Awards—not as grizzly as Bob Dylan, who beat her in the soundtrack category, nor as extraordinarily ordinary as Julia "Golly!" Roberts, who beat her in the best-actress category, but a thick-eyebrowed beauty amid all the tinsel and thin.

And then there were the Oscars. For the celebrity ritual known as Hollywood's biggest night, when as much attention is paid to which actress is wearing which designer's dress as to the content of the movies awarded—for the yearly red-carpet gauntlet that superstars spend months agonizing over—Björk showed up wearing a swan.

It was a priceless moment, one that won her, ironically, more attention in the States than her actual performance in *Dancer in the Dark* did. Amid Julia "I don't have a stylist" Roberts bragging about her "vintage Valentino" and all the "Versace this" and "Gucci that," the Icelandic iconoclast wore a simple, sleeveless party frock with a stuffed animal sewn into it. When an interviewer on the pre-awards telecast commented on the dress's unusualness, Björk, stroking the swan's head, replied, "Thank you. My friend made it."

What *is* this thing called Björk?

After I had already turned in the first draft of this book, but before the Academy Awards ceremony, I met up with Björk again in person at Elektra's New York headquarters while on assignment for *Interview* magazine. The following quotes are outtakes from that conversation. At that point—March 2, 2001—*Vespertine* was scheduled to come out in May. Having spent a couple of months immersed in her music, statements, and films, I was extremely nervous about meeting Björk in the flesh again. Would she live up to the conception I had formed? What if this woman in whom I had found a certain modern, even future, ideal turned out to be a bitch?

Björk was nervous too. "I haven't done this for ages," she apologized halfway through. "So I'm drinking a lot of coffee and just motormouthing it." Indeed, she had two cappuccino-looking brews in paper cups in front of her, both partially drunk. After making her little, unnecessary apology, she proceeded to place one cup in the other, spilling coffee across the table. She seemed shakier, but in a way friendlier, than last time we had met. Her head and neck pulsed with minuscule tics, as if she were a small animal in a vulnerable position alert for predators. Her tongue repeatedly darted out to take a full 360-degree lap around her lips, then slipped back in, as if her mouth couldn't stand being caged in this dry conference room. A twitcher myself, I felt at ease—or at least in familiar company.

Once again, Björk proved to be more forward-thinking than even her fascinating music would indicate. I had been given five songs from the album now named *Vespertine,* meaning literally "of vespers (evening prayers)" but more broadly referring to anything to do with evening, such as flowers that bloom after dusk. The tracks are more orchestral, softer and more melancholy, than anything she has done before. Rather than being beat- or melody-driven, the music moves in ripples and waves. If Björk had laid herself out emotionally on *Homogenic,* on *Vespertine* she shows her "Hidden Place."

As ever, Björk expresses the emotional quality of technological advance, finding the personal, human poetry in digital life—future shack, not future shock. "Most of the album is done on a laptop," she explained. "I've never done an album in as many locations as this one: in bedrooms and offices and trailers and film sets and hotel rooms and friends' houses. It goes with what the album's about: to create a paradise anywhere you go. It's very based on the home, indoors. *Homogenic* was made in quite a steroid, sort of fueled experience—really boosted, with the beats on eleven, and distorted, emotionally distorted too, everything overemotional, very violent, as dramatic as you can get. This the reverse, in that it's all about reaching euphoric highs by whispering. The whole sound level of this album, instead of being like a concert with stacks of speakers blasting it out, it's more about the situation we're in, me and you, now. I would open my laptop and do a little tune, and then I would just stand up and sing for you. . . .

"It's kind of how a hundred years ago you had people having string quartets and playing harpsichords entertain each other in the evening—the family members, doing some knitting or whatever. I think we've gone full cycle and now we can do that again, but with laptops, and people playing computer games. Or, say Dad is obsessed with trout-fishing, he can go in the Internet and research that. And then me mum is into death metal, and she can download some Napster stuff. I see that sort of thing a lot more than ten years ago, with my friends. It's such a short cut: People don't have to physically go all over the planet to make their dreams come true. They can do it in their kitchen. That's what this album is attempting to deal with: To make a paradise in kitchens—that's the ultimate, that's the ideal musical experience. That's where it's gonna happen, and luckily enough, it's the same place that your heart is."

In recording *Vespertine,* Björk used volumes and timbres that would sound good coming out of a personal computer's small speakers. This is music you can carry with you and hold on your lap. Ironically, this sonic quest led her back to classical European instruments: harp and celesta (the glockenspiel-like tiny piano used by Tchaikovsky in *The Nutcracker Suite*). Elsewhere, there's a sixty-piece orchestra. "Cocoon" opens with little synthesizer scratches—"microbeats," Björk calls them—that sound like analog pops and crackles, like a needle on an old record. Björk's voice enters similarly raw and unprocessed, as if she's singing in your ear, all intaken breaths and quivering, sung exhales, the spit on tonsils nearly audible. The lyrics are direct and erotic, describing falling asleep after sex then awakening with her lover still inside her: "gorgeousness."

Having mastered the techno musical, Björk is creating electronic chamber music. She plans to perform the new material in opera halls, without mikes and amplifiers. "I first thought that [the idea of] opera houses was pretty snotty. But in Europe, they spent years and years making the acoustics magical, so you can actually whisper and it sounds gorgeous. It's how I learned to sing, because I would just walk outside all the time, that's how I developed my voice. Then when I started singing in bands, I felt compromised, 'cause you only put a certain percentage of your voice through a microphone. So much is about the sensitivities that get lost. I think that's one of the reasons why my songs differ on this album, because there's so much room for all the hairs and all the little delicate things. Usually, these sensitivities get bulldozed over."

After her London explosion, Björk is still in introspective retreat mode. On the new songs, she's frequently trying to cope. "If you wake up and the day feels broken, Just lead into the crack," she philosophizes on "It's Not Up to You," speaking from personal experience. The tone of the album was in many ways set by her *Dancer* days. Writing songs in the evening was her way of dealing with the stress of the shoot. Her laptop became her audio journal.

"When I was doing the film, working on this album was almost like having an affair," she told me. "You were doing it on the side. You would be in the evenings in the hotel room, with your laptop. I could do long shoot days and come home really really tired, and I would use it to record a tune, just my own stuff, just to cut it out, and then I would go and sleep peacefully and wake up ready for the next day."

Other songs capture the first passionate flush of love, in frank, erotic detail. Björk won't talk about her personal life, but sources say she's dating Matthew Barney, a controversial performance artist who named his most notorious film after the muscle that controls the raising and lowering of testicles. If true, it's another fabulously adventurous coupling for Björk. She did tell me that for the last year, she has spent more time in New York—where Barney lives—than out if it. She loves New York, spends her time walking across its steel and concrete bridges and singing into traffic. "I'm obsessed with the bridges," she said. "They are pretty powerful, aren't they? You can walk back and forth on them, and you can sing at the top of your lungs because nobody's there really. And it's extreme, where nature and man are trying to have a handshake."

Strange: I wrote this book a stone's throw away from the Manhattan Bridge, looking out my Brooklyn office window at the parade of vans across its steel spans.

Even stranger is that as Björk was making her album to be heard on a laptop, I was writing this book to be read as a digital file. When she described the way creating—or really, communicating—on a computer feels intensely internal and private, like entering a secret garden with intimates, I knew exactly what she meant. "It's like a world that hasn't got oxygen and wind and water," she said. "It's very similar to how we dream and how we are on the inside. It's like those paintings by the surrealists about dreams, all these landscapes, but they never had any oxygen in them. That's the sort of landscapes that are in our imagination."

This ability to burrow deep into her constantly curious, unique mind and pull out something wholly unexpected is what makes Björk so brilliant—and kooky. I mean, what was she thinking, wearing a swan to the Oscars? It was vintage Björk, really: child-like, playful, "quirky." It was the sensational fruit of her latest collaboration with an experimental designer: The "friend" who made the dress was Marjan Pejoski, who also designed the pink dress Björk wore at Cannes. At the Oscars, Björk carried four eggs made by Pejoski that she kept leaving in various places, only to have them returned to her by bemused film-industry personnel.

Björk was pulling the ultimate surrealist prank. She had vowed *Dancer* would be her last movie, so performing "I've Seen It All" on the Oscars telecast was her swan song—get it? For her actual performance, she wound up ditching the once-planned Thom Yorke duet and the elaborate stage set the show's producers had created. Instead, she just sang, alone on the stage except for a man on synthesizers in the background, with the orchestra in the pit—just her and her swan, singing methodically, tremulously, forgetting the words at one point in her nervousness, very un-Hollywood, simultaneously surreal and very real.

Of course, many people thought she was weird as hell. The Academy Awards, created to honor the best, bring out Hollywood's worst: Joan Rivers and all the nattering nabobs of negativity dragging out their cattiest, cruelest, most conservative remarks—as if they thought Björk were serious.

Still, seeing her so nervous on stage, remembering the tics and the spilt coffee, knowing how hard it is to be the brave weirdo, to show up wearing the wonderful garment you found only to have everyone laugh at you, I was glad she had a swan to pet.

It's not easy being different. Björk may be representing for us musicaholic-impaired introverts, doing her rescue thing for the Selmas of the world. But way back in 1987, she told Chris Roberts for *Melody Maker,* "It's so painful to hear that I'm a freak in people's eyes. I am twenty-one years old and I have been fighting all my life for being looked at as normal. I am just normal to me."

By 2001, Björk was more confident, more aware of the unconventions she had chosen. "I have a very peculiar inbred system in me; I don't know who put it there, I was born with it I guess," she told me. "I put a record out when I was eleven and that went big in Iceland, and I freaked out. And they asked me to do another one and I was like *nn-nn* [shakes head]. And then I did one punk band, and that started to become big when I was fourteen, and I was earning more money than my mum, just in punk gigs. And then I quit that and started the cult experimental anarchy sort of terrorist Einstürzende Neubauten band, so it was always pretty definite I could piss everybody off. This idea of being massive is not necessarily appealing to me. I always look at it like if you see a class in school, like how kids are? I'm definitely not your natural cheerleader. I'm more the eccentric in the back. And I feel comfortable there."

But Björk doesn't stay in the back. She puts her eccentric self front and center.

It's extremely difficult to talk about art without getting all pretentious, something that, like Björk, I'm loath to be. I'd like to try to convey the incredible pain and daring involved in creating something where there was nothing and then surrendering it to the world—I think it's a lot like parenting. I suspect, in fact, it's the mother in Björk that wants happy endings, for Selma, for everyone—most of her albums end with songs of hope. "Joy is the hardest thing to put across," U2 singer Bono says on the Bravo biography of Björk. Maybe what's most important about Björk is that she conveys joy in a way that's not smiley-face simple, but fierce and dangerous and complex—"Violently Happy," as she puts it. I hope you don't have to be an artist to appreciate that. I like to think everyone has a spark of the unquenched individuality that erupts from Björk like a volcano—that every ugly duckling has a swan inside of her.

Björk, Year by Year

1965: Björk Gudmundsdóttir, daughter of Hildur Hauksdóttir and Gudmundur Gunnarsson, is born on November 21 in Reykjavík, Iceland.

1967: Hildur and Gudmundur divorce.

1970: Hildur marries guitarist Saevar Arnason. Four-year-old Björk begins writing songs.

1972: Björk enrolls at Baramusikskola Reykjavíkur, a music school, where she studies recorder, piano, and flute. The band Sparks releases its album *Kimono My House*, the first record Björk owned.

1977: *Björk Gudmundsdóttir*, the singer's debut (not to be confused with the much later *Debut*), is released in the autumn. The psychedelic cover is designed by Hildur.

1979: Björk joins her first band, playing drums for the all-female punk ensemble Spit & Snot.

1980: Björk joins her second band, the prog-rocky Exodus.

1981: Björk returns to a more punk sound with Tappi Tíkarrass (literally, "a cork in a bitch's ass," a charming Icelandic saying for something that fits well). Tappi appears in the 1982 rockumentary *Rock in Reykjavík*.

1982: Björk falls in love for the first time, with guitarist Thor Eldon. She moves in with him that evening. She also meets poet Sigurjón B. Sigurdsson (aka Sjón), Einar Örn, and other members of Iceland's poetry posse Medusa.

1983: Tappi breaks up and Björk joins Kukl, an Icelandic punk supergroup whose name means "witch." Members are

Einar Örn, Einar Melax, Gulli Ottarsson (a.k.a. God Krist), Sigtryggur "Siggi" Baldursson, and Birgir Mogensen (also spelled Morgensen, according to some sources).

1984: Kukl's first album, *The Eye*, is released by British anarchist outfit Crass's record label.

1985: Kukl's second album, *Holidays in Europe (The Naughty Nought)*, is released. The band breaks up that year.

1986: Björk gives birth to her son, Sindri, on June 8. By this point she and Thor are married. Thor and Einar Örn form Bad Taste Records, a collective inspired by Picasso's saying, "The worst enemy of creativity is good taste." Members of Bad Taste form a band that plays its first show in August, as Pukl; the group subsequently changes its name to the Sugarcubes.

1987: Björk makes her acting debut, starring in the Icelandic film *The Juniper Tree*. In September, the Sugarcubes' first single, "Birthday," is released in Britain. *Melody Maker* proclaims it single of the year. By this time, Thor and Björk have split.

1988: The Sugarcubes' debut, *Life's Too Good*, is released. The band tours the United States for the first time and plays *Saturday Night Live*.

1989: The Sugarcubes tour America with Public Image Ltd. and New Order on the Monsters of Alternative Rock tour. Their second album, *Here Today, Tomorrow, Next Week*, is released and the backlash, most of it directed against Örn, begins.

1990: The Sugarcubes tour the world. On December 9 Einar Örn and Bragi Ólafsson wed in Copenhagen.

1991: *Gling-Gló*, Björk's recording with Trio Gudmundar Ingólfssonar, is released by Bad Taste in Iceland. Her two tracks recorded with 808 State are released on that group's *Ex:El* album.

1992: The Sugarcubes' *Stick Around for Joy* is released. The band tours the United States with U2. On November 17, they decide not to stick around, playing their final show at the Limelight in New York.

1993: Björk settles in London and releases *Debut*. She performs for the first time with her new multinational band in London in August, wearing a paper dress by Hussein Chalayan.

1994: Björk performs with PJ Harvey at the Brit Awards and plays model for Jean–Paul Gaultier at the spring shows in Paris. She performs on *MTV Unplugged* with saxophonist Oliver Lake, deaf percussionist Evelyn Glennie, a gamelan orchestra, and octogenarian harpist Corky Hale. After Madonna asks Björk and Nellee Hooper to produce her next album, Björk writes her the song "Bedtime Story."

1995: Björk wins Brits for Best Female and International Artist. She begins collaborating (ahem) with Tricky. She records *Post* on the beach in the Bahamas with Hooper, Marius De Vries, and Howie B.

1996: On February 19, Björk assaults a TV reporter in Bangkok. Björk and Goldie get engaged. *Telegram* is released. The British post office intercepts a letter bomb sent to Björk by a fan in Florida who subsequently commits suicide. Tricky and Goldie get into a fistfight at a New York club in Björk's presence.

1997: I fly to Iceland to interview Björk on the eve of the release of *Homogenic*.

1999: Lars von Trier begins filming *Dancer in the Dark*.

2000: In June Björk wins the best performance award at Cannes for her role in *Dancer*. The film and *Selmasongs* are released in the United States that fall. Björk is nominated for two Golden Globe awards: best actress and best song.

2001: Björk is nominated for two Grammies and an Oscar. She performs on the Oscars telecast wearing a swan. Her first self-produced album, *Vespertine*, is released in August.

Record by Record

Note: With a couple of exceptions (such as her 1977 debut), for simplicity's sake this discography lists only Björk's U.S. releases. All are released by Elektra Records unless otherwise noted. It is as comprehensive as I could manage without going completely Bjonkers. There are many songs by Björk on compilation and soundtrack albums, and she has collaborated with artists too numerous to mention.

ALBUMS, SOLO

1977: *Björk Gudmundsdóttir* (out-of-print album originally released only in Iceland)
1. Arabadrengurinn
2. Bukolla
3. Alta Mira
4. Johannes Kjarval
5. Fusi Hreindyr
6. Himnafor
7. Oliver
8. Alfur Ut Ur Hol
9. Musastiginn
10. Baenin

1990: *Gling-Gló* (One Little Indian), with Trio Gudmundar Ingólfssonar
　　1. Gling–Gló
　　2. Luktar–Gvendur
　　3. Kata Rokkar
　　4. Pabbi Minn
　　5. Brestir Og Brak
　　6. Ástartöfrar
　　7. Bella Símamaer
　　8. Litli Tónlistarmadurinn
　　9. Pad Sést Ekki Saetari Mey
　　10. Bílavísur
　　11. Tondeleyo
　　12. Ég Veit Ei Hvad Skal Segja
　　13. Í Dansi Med Thér
　　14. Börnin Vid Tjörnina
　　15. Ruby Baby
　　16. I Can't Help Loving That Man

1993: *Debut*
　　1. Human Behaviour
　　2. Crying
　　3. Venus as a Boy
　　4. There's More to Life than This
　　5. Like Someone in Love
　　6. Big Time Sensuality
　　7. One Day
　　8. Aeroplane
　　8. Come to Me
　　9. Violently Happy
　　10. The Anchor Song

1995: *Post*
　　1. Army of Me
　　2. Hyper–ballad
　　3. The Modern Things

4. It's Oh So Quiet
5. Enjoy
6. You've Been Flirting Again
7. Isobel
8. Possibly Maybe
9. I Miss You
10. Cover Me
11. Headphones

1996: *Telegram*
1. Possibly Maybe (remixed by LFO)
2. Hyper-ballad (remixed by Brodsky Quartet)
3. Enjoy (remixed by Outcast)
4. My Spine (with Evelyn Glennie)
5. I Miss You (remixed by Dobie)
6. Isobel (remixed by Deodato)
7. You've Been Flirting Again (remixed by Björk)
8. Cover Me (remixed by Dillinja)
9. Army of Me (remixed by Graham Massey)
10. Headphones (remixed by Mika Vainio)
11. I Miss You

1997: *Homogenic*
1. Hunter
2. Jóga
3. Unravel
4. Bachelorette
5. All Neon Like
6. 5 Years
7. Immature
8. Alarm Call
9. Pluto
10. All Is Full of Love

2000: *Selmasongs*
1. Overture

2. Cvalda
3. I've Seen It All
4. Scatterheart
5. In the Musicals
6. 107 Steps
7. New World

ALBUMS, WITH KUKL

1984: *The Eye* (Crass Records)
1. Assassin
2. Moonbath
3. The Spire
4. Anna
5. Dismembered
6. Seagull

1985: *Holidays in Europe (The Naughty Nought)* (Crass Records) (no
tracks listed on CD)

ALBUMS, WITH THE SUGARCUBES

1988: *Life's Too Good*
1. Traitor
2. Motorcrash
3. Birthday
4. Delicious Demon
5. Mama
6. Coldsweat
7. Blue Eyed Pop
8. Deus
9. Sick for Toys
10. F***ing in Rhythm *&* Sorrow
11. Take Some Petrol Darling

12. Cowboy*
13. I Want...*
14. Dragon (Icelandic)*
15. Cat (Icelandic)*
16. Coldsweat (remix)*
17. Deus (remix)*

*CD tracks not on original release

1989: *Here Today, Tomorrow, Next Week!*

1. Tidal Wave
2. Regina
3. Speed Is the Key
4. Dream TV
5. Nail
6. Pump
7. Eat the Menu
8. The Bee
9. Dear Plastic
10. Shoot Him
11. Water
12. A Day Called Zero
13. Planet
14. Hey*
15. Dark Disco*
16. Hot Meat*

*CD tracks not on original release

1992: *Stick Around for Joy*

1. Gold
2. Hit
3. Leash Called Love
4. Lucky Night
5. Happy Nurse
6. I'm Hungry
7. Walkabout
8. Hetero Scum

9. Vitamin
10. Chihuahua

SUGARCUBES COMPILATIONS

1992: *It's-It*
1. Birthday (Justin Robertson 12″ mix)
2. Leash Called Love (Tony Humphries mix)
3. Blue Eyed Pop (S 1000 mix)
4. Motorcrash (Justin Robertson mix)
5. Planet (Graham Massey Planet Suite Pt. 2)
6. Gold (Todd Terry mix)
7. Water (Bryan "Chuck" New mix)
8. Regina (Sugarcubes mix)
9. Mama (Mark Saunders mix)
10. Pump (Marius De Vries mix)
11. Hit (Tony Humphries Sweet & Low mix)
12. Birthday (Tommy D mix)
13. Coldsweat (DB/BP mix)

1998: *The Great Crossover Potential*
1. Birthday
2. Cold Sweat
3. Mama
4. Motorcrash
5. Deus
6. Regina
7. Pump
8. Planet
9. Water
10. Hit
11. Vitamin
12. Walkabout
13. Gold
14. Chihuahua

SINGLES

1993: Human Behaviour
Violently Happy
Venus as a Boy [#1]
Venus as a Boy [#2]
1994: Big Time Sensuality
1995: It's Oh So Quiet
1997: I Miss You/Cover Me
Hyper–ballad/Enjoy
1998: Hunter
1999: Alarm Call Part 1
Alarm Call Part 2
Alarm Call Part 3
All Is Full of Love

FILMS

1987: *The Juniper Tree*
1994: *Ready to Wear (Prêt-à-Porter)*
2000: *Dancer in the Dark*

VIDEOS

1994: *Vessel*
1998: *Live at Shepherd's Bush Empire*
Volumen
1999: *All Is Full of Love*

Acknowledgments

When Jonathan Karp first approached me about writing an e-book for Random House, I wasn't sure what he was talking about. I'm still not sure what this is, but Jonathan is so supportive and such a true lover of writing—and of writing that veers outside the lines— I've been happy to come along. When Jonathan took a little detour in his own career, the wonderful Janelle Duryea stepped in, happy to share her love of Björk, along with Mary Bahr. Thanks to all of them.

My agent, Sarah Lazin, with the help of Paula Balzar, performed the thankless task of trying to sort out the legal and financial questions of what an e-book is. They worked incredibly hard for little reward, and I'm very grateful.

Sherry Ring, Iris Tesson, Scott Rogers, and Stuart Green all helped me in matters Björkian. Joel Amsterdam at Elektra set up my 1997 interview with Björk, thus setting this book in motion. Susan Hamre, then editor at *Request,* had the incredibly good sense to assign and publish that interview. Thanks to Joel, Susan, Elektra, and *Request* for the trip to Iceland!

Scott Cohen at *Interview* magazine sent me to chat with Björk again in 2001. Thanks to him, Ingrid Sischy, Brad Goldfarb, Dimitri Ehrlich, Graham Fuller, Patrick Giles, Kathy Campbell, Sean Kennedy, and Chrissy Persico for creating a great work environment.

Thanks to the Fictionaires, Vivien Goldman and Jana Martin, for helping me with my nonfiction too. I miss you!

Thanks to Ray Rogers for everything you've done—you're the man!

Thanks to Cathay Che, Vickie Starr, Mike Tyler, Brian Parks, Meg Handler, Dina Suggs, Christopher Johnson, Paul Rubin, Sara Valentine, Cindy Pederson, Jeff Weiss, Debbi Gibbs, and Kate Giel for all the good conversation, meals, parties, sojourns, thoughts, and just plain good times.

Mom, Dad, Brett: Love always.

Love to Bud, Karlie, Kenda, Elvis, God (she's a cat), and Otis—my family.

And, of course, thanks to Björk for never leaving me at a loss for inspiration.

Evelyn McDonnell's Suggested Websites

The official Björk website, and an excellent source of info as well as odd-ball animation, is www.bjork.com/unity. The official record company website for Björk is www.elektra.com/retro/bjork/index.html.

Information on, and CDs and videos by, Björk and the Sugarcubes can be found at ubl.artistdirect.com.

There is a good site called, yes, www.TheSugarcubes.com.

Information on Björk's early music as part of the obscure Kukl can be found at www.southern.com/southern/band/KUKLL and at www.larvik.folkebibl.no/~vidar/musikk/kukl.html.

Go to www.dancerinthedark.com to find out more about the movie.

To find out more about the Vow of Chastity, go to www.dogme95.dk.

For a bio of Lars von Trier, go to us.imdb.com/Bio?von+Trier,+Lars.

About the Author

After twelve years in New York City, EVELYN MCDONNELL recently moved to Miami, where she is the pop-music critic at *The Miami Herald*. Her cultural criticism has been published in periodicals including *Interview, Ms., Rolling Stone, Spin, Out, The New York Times*, and *Request*, as well as in several collections. A former music editor at *The Village Voice* and *San Francisco Weekly*, she has coedited two anthologies: *Rock She Wrote: Women Write About Rock, Pop, and Rap* (Cooper Square) and *Stars Don't Stand Still in the Sky: Music and Myth* (Dia/NYU Press). She also wrote the history of the musical *Rent* that was published with the libretto by Rob Weisbach Books/William Morrow.

About AtRandom.com Books

AtRandom.com Books, a new imprint within the Random House Trade Group, is dedicated to publishing original books that harness the power of new technologies. Each title, commissioned expressly for this publishing program, will be offered simultaneously in various digital formats and as a trade paperback.

AtRandom.com books are designed to provide people with choices about their reading experience and the information they can obtain. They are aimed at communities of highly motivated readers who want immediate access to substantive and artful writing on the various subjects that fascinate them.

Our list features expert writing on health, business, technology, culture, entertainment, law, finance, and a variety of other topics. Whether written in a spirit of play, rigorous critique, or practical instruction, these books possess a vitality that new ways of publishing can aptly serve.

For information about AtRandom.com Books and to sign up for our e-newsletters, visit www.atrandom.com.